Dollars and Scholars

*An Inquiry into the Impact of Faculty
Income Upon the Function and Future
of the Academy*

Robert H. Linnell
Editor

Library of Congress Catalog Card Number: 82-051020

Copyright © 1982 by

       The University of Southern California Press
       Student Union 404
       University of Southern California
       Los Angeles, CA 90089

ISBN Number: 0-88474-106-0

CONTENTS

(Supported by a grant from the
Carnegie Corporation of New York)

ACKNOWLEDGMENTS

This monograph serves as the final summary report of the *Ethical and Economic Issues Project of the University of Southern California*. The project was made possible by an initial planning grant and, later, a project grant from the Carnegie Corporation of New York. The authors sincerely appreciate not only this financial support but also the insights and encouragement of Alden Dunham, the Carnegie Project Officer.

This project has had the benefit of an exceptionally knowledgeable and dedicated advisory committee; the topics of this study are wide-ranging and sensitive. The issues discussed are certain to evoke spirited response in any group of academics, and our advisory committee was no exception. This monograph benefited greatly from the ideas and critical reactions of this diverse and experienced group. Responsibility for the analyses and opinions in the final monograph must rest however with the authors alone.

Advisory Committee Members

Edward Blakely, University of California, Systemwide Administration
Donald F. Costello, University of Nebraska
Henry B. Clark, University of Southern California
*Louis Levin, National Science Foundation (retired)
Paul Olum, University of Oregon
John C. Weaver, University of Southern California
Raymond J. Woodrow, Princeton University
John T. Wilson, University of Chicago

*Deceased, March 11, 1981

This book is dedicated to the memory of Louis Levin. He set an example of integrity and steadfast effort for the betterment of society. His personal interests were always secondary to the greater good and what he believed to be right. His support and inspiration continue in the lives of those who had the privilege to know and work with him.

Robert H. Linnell

AUTHORS AND EDITORS

Clarence N. Anderson, University Editor at USC, read the entire manuscript. His understanding of the academy and his writing skills were of great help.

Henry B. Clark is Professor of Religion and Associate Director, USC Center for the Humanities.

Terry L. Cooper, Assistant Professor of Public Administration, made significant contribution to Chapter 2.

Zoe L. Cosgrove, former Information Coordinator at USC, read seemingly endless manuscript drafts with patience and diligence and provided much needed editing.

Donald F. Costello, on leave as Director of Academic Computer Services, the University of Nebraska and currently Senior Management Consultant at Tulane University, provided many ideas for Chapter 6. The development of the concept of an Office of Intellectual Property Management and the importance of copyrightable computer center products are essentially his work.

We thank Ed Cray, Senior Lecturer at the USC School of Journalism, for his professional editorial assistance which clarified our writing and made the entire monograph more readable.

Kristine E. Dillon was Research Associate and later Associate Director of the USC Ethical and Economic Issues Project. She is currently Associate Director of Management Information and Studies, USC Office of the University Budget.

Robert H. Linnell was Director of the USC Ethical and Economic Issues Project. He has been Director of the USC Office of Institutional Studies and is currently Professor of Safety and Chemistry.

Clark McCartney, Director of the USC Office of Patent and Copyright Administration, reviewed and contributed to Chapter 6.

We also owe thanks to many others who read chapters, provided ideas and helped to clarify the thinking and writing of the authors.

Robert H. Linnell, Editor
University of Southern California
Los Angeles, California
June 1982

Preface

Flushed with two decades of unprecedented growth and afflu-
ence, the academic world confronts a future of straitened finances
and lower enrollments with more apprehension than vision. An
anxious self-interest has crept into the academy, accompanied by
a sense of frustration and drift. The vitality of education and
scholarship, the mainspring of social change just a decade ago,
has flagged.

Challenged, even disparaged by the very people who have most
benefited from its heritage, the academy remains essential to
shaping and nourishing meaningful lives. An over-populated and
resource-depleted planet requires emphasis on the intellectual
and esthetic, an optimal use of resources with less exploitive
waste of diminishing natural resources. Although material resources of *Planet Earth* are finite, human resource potential continues indefinitely, and herein lies the great opportunity for education. We work with the limitless human resource, and the
constraints of material resources or finances need not deter us in
the years ahead.

Accountability, flexibility, and ability to grow and change,
these are the characteristics demanded of academe in the coming
decades. Yet it is easy to find evidence that institutions of higher
education are the most rigid and change-resistant organizations
to be found in our society.

We sense that colleges and universities are falling far short of
the lofty goals they have set and that we are all thus diminished.
A major problem is that most faculty are paid on the old agrarian
nine-month basis (in reality a three-fourths part-time position)
and that these academic salaries lag behind inflation rates. To

keep pace, the vast majority (80 to 90 percent) of faculty engage in additional remunerative work, much of it professionally related. This in turn has fostered the potential for conflict-of-interest; moreover, developments in such fast-moving, potentially lucrative technologies as gene-splicing and computers are creating serious problems for the maintenance of academic freedom.

Any study combining ethics and economics is bound to provoke vigorous controversy. During the course of this work we have received much correspondence, most of it encouraging, yet some very negative.

The dean of faculty of a major institution wrote:

> As to your question as to whether the fragmented sources of earnings make it difficult for faculty to exercise their best talents as teachers and scholars, I would phrase it somewhat differently. I think that in many instances these extra earnings seduce the faculty away from their best teaching and scholarship.

A senior administrator of one of the most prestigious universities wrote:

> The problem area is really a region in which there are many separate problems. The problem of intellectual property, for example, has, despite its long history, significant conceptual gaps on which scholars are currently at work. Consulting is all by itself an aggregation of issues that differ depending on the discipline . . . the diversity of issues seems impossible to capture in a single study. Another type of diversity . . . is the diversity of institutions. Another point of departure has to do with the current political climate. A broad scale study of the type you propose might start an inquisition, over-running the many traditional and legitimate forms of incentive and latitude open to faculty members. That's always a danger with large examinations. But when the atmosphere is highly charged, the danger magnifies. If that should happen, the study would lose its chance of making an intelligent contribution equal to the magnitude of the problem. In short, I think such a study as you propose could impair rather than enhance pluralism in higher education.

We requested salary data (base salaries and overbase payments), policy information and case histories illustrating conflict-of-interest problems. We made a strong commitment to confidentiality of institutional and individual identity. While most recipients of our survey cooperated, for which we were grateful, there were many refusals. In the conflict-of-interest area we were faced with an almost complete lack of cooperation. Campus interviews seemed to indicate that everyone had some experience with conflict-of-interest cases but we were unable to obtain a single written case history. This is unfortunate, because we feel that analysis of a number of well-documented case histories would be useful in developing more adequate policy and procedure.

One of our studies was titled "Total University Earnings at Research Universities," in which useable data were obtained from 12 institutions. We proposed to extend this study to all 168 research and doctoral institutions and some 30 did agree to provide data. An astonishingly large number of institutions stated that they did not know the total salary paid their faculty. A few refused to participate based on principle, as indicated by one administrator in a state university:

> Some indication of total salaries earned by faculty members is of interest to me . . . In spite of this interest I would *not* support the creation of a new national data base of such salaries . . . I fear the excessive publication of such data . . . could easily be used as political ammunition to deny appropriations for faculty salary increases at a time when these (and other) salaries are losing ground to inflation. Thus, I find your current study of interest, but I feel the dangers outweigh the benefits of further work on the topic.

Another respondent (from a state university) to the total institutional salary study wrote:

> Let me offer congratulations upon having developed a most important statement . . . Unfortunately, the timing for making such a shift in assembling and reporting academic salaries may prove damaging. When there is widespread public pressure for reducing higher education spending, reporting that, all along, faculty have been earning much more than has been indicated, would, in my judgment, further erode public confidence in educational leadership.

Some wrote of other concerns. A state university dean confided:

> There are many of us in higher education who are the products of industry and business and who have, for some time, been warning our peers that the comfortable lack of accountability to the taxpayer and, indeed, to the student will someday come to rest on our shoulders with a heavy, heavy weight. I only wish that faculty would read your newsletter and take it seriously, but it is the very lack of accountability which will cause them not to do so. This makes me sad.

We have tried to secure objective data and to collect as many opinions and case histories as possible. The reluctance to admit to problems, the complexities of the issues and the real (usually strongly held) differences of opinions have made it difficult. We admit that our own opinions indicate major problems and generally weak university action. We are willing to take responsibility for any shortcomings of our work. The conclusions and recommendations are ultimately our own although we are greatly indebted to many others and, most importantly to an advisory committee. Some readers will certainly disagree with us. We hope our efforts will add to the discussions which will lead ultimately to new policies and toward realizing the ideals upon which the academy is founded.

Robert H. Linnell

1. Ethical and Economic Issues Facing Academe in a Rapidly Changing Society

Robert H. Linnell

IN 1908 HENRY PRITCHETT, then President of the Carnegie Foundation for the Advancement of Teaching, described the economic state of the academic profession by stating:

A large proportion of the teachers in American Universities are engaged in turning to the grindstone of some outside employment with one hand whilst they carry on the work of the teacher with the other. Owing to the rise in the cost of living the proportion of teachers who seek to increase their incomes in this way is very large. The method of organization of the American university also throws a large amount of executive work upon members of the faculty. For this, extra compensation is sometimes paid. Both pressures cut down the opportunity of scholarly study and take away from the dignity, simplicity, and high-mindedness of the teacher's calling . . . However advantageous it may be for a professor to engage in outside expert work, this should be, like his private research, an opportunity which he can accept or decline according to his own judgment. Extra-university employment should never be forced upon teachers by a salary schedule arranged on a part-time basis. College and university teaching is sufficient to employ to its full capacity the energy of a single mind. . . For the college departments and the graduate scholars of a university to entrust the instruction of their students to professors or instructors who are compelled to give to teaching only part of their ability and attention is an unwise policy. The students must inevitably suffer.[1]

This monograph deals with ethical and economic issues important to the future of higher education, even as they were to Pritchett 74 years ago. Yet they remain largely ignored, or worse, deliberately brushed under the rug as troubling, or potentially disruptive of tradition. Examining the various ways by which academic salaries are paid and faculty members garner supplemental income, this study examines the possible ethical issues associated with each of these sources of income and their impact on the three primary functions of the academy: transmission of knowledge, creation of new knowledge and art forms, and public service.

The primary focus is on the academic faculty, for the faculty role is unique. Academic freedom and tenure, the academic work year, modest scheduled class hours, and generally flexible work hours set faculty apart from other university employees, indeed, from most employees in America. Furthermore, the faculty marketplace has now changed and once generous university budgets have diminished alarmingly. During the tremendous growth period of 1950-1970, the competition for scarce or outstanding faculty forced salaries rapidly upward (base academic salaries outpaced the cost of living by approximately 65 percent from 1948/49 to 1967/68). Fringe benefits multiplied, promotions and tenure came relatively rapidly and easily, and teaching loads declined. The recent abrupt change in enrollment growth, coupled with double-digit inflation and a surplus of qualified candidates for faculty positions, has radically altered the academic job market. For the last several years base academic salaries have lagged behind cost-of-living increases by more than 2 percent per year, creating financial strains that have increased the pressures on faculty members to seek supplemental income.[2]

At the same time there is an increasing public interest in accountability: do these faculty supplemental income activities come at the expense of the academic responsibilities for which faculty are paid? Academics vaguely defend such activities as a benefit to society, asserting that abuses are rare. However, the diffuse definition of faculty workloads and general lack of enforceable codes of conduct make it almost impossible for higher education to rebut the growing criticism.

Even if a great deal more research is being done in academe than in Pritchett's day, his statement of 74 years ago is still remarkably appropriate! Under today's economy the need for supplemental income is urgent, and faculty involvement in such work has increased considerably in recent years. A 1962 survey[3] indicated that 13 percent of the faculty at four-year colleges and universities received outside consulting fees, whereas in the 1975 Ladd-Lipset survey[4] the corresponding number was 48 percent. The same 1975 survey indicated that 89 percent of all faculty earned some supplemental income. Though a few do not earn supplemental income—for lack of opportunity, by choice or principle—clearly supplemental income is of significant importance to most faculty today. Most faculty today are, in effect, (and by appointment letter or contract) part-time employees; their teaching appointments are for three-quarters of a year (nine-months). Furthermore, the policy of most institutions permits or encourages consulting or other extra-university work which can result in a four-day (or sometimes less) campus work week during that nine-month appointment.

THE ACADEMY AND SOCIETY

Higher education writings and the popular press provide abundant material related to ethical and economic issues which are of concern. For example, a recent Carnegie study[5] states:

> Colleges and universities have taught and practiced moral and civic virtues throughout our national history, have sought to advance the truth, and have been devoted to public service. Their members often have served as the conscience of the nation. The academic virtues are a model for the conduct of society at large. They include respect for facts and careful analysis; civility in argument; careful consideration of alternative points of view and solutions to problems; and reliance on persuasion.

The report continues:

> We are concerned about the prospective frantic search by many faculty members, many departments, and many colleges for scarce students in the 1980's and 1990's. Unless corrective actions are taken, such conditions are likely to lead some students to try to take even greater advantage of the situation, and to make some colleges even more reluctant to insist on ethical conduct by students and even more likely to engage in improper conduct themselves. We are concerned that these negative behavioral traits may indicate a larger and more deep-seated problem: a general loss of self-confidence and sense of mutual trust, and a general decline in integrity of conduct on campus. The basic problem may be bigger than the sum of its component parts. "Rip-offs" and excessive "legalisms" are bad in themselves, but worse for what they imply about the general situation. One evidence of the latter is increased litigiousness. Already there has been clear erosion of public respect for some aspects of the conduct of some individuals and some institutions. This erosion of respect is one basis for erosion of support, and for the increasing and alarming loss of institutional autonomy. It does some good to

acknowledge them and to seek to correct them. Whether or not ethical conduct has deteriorated to a significant degree in some areas of campus activities, and we are convinced that in some ways it is clearly less defensible, we are concerned that there is more scrutiny of campus conduct by students, by the public, by the states, by the federal government, and by the press. As a consequence of this, it is at least prudent for a campus to give prior scrutiny to itself.

Another example is an address to the Second National Conference on Business Ethics, in which Senator Mark O. Hatfield called for an "ethical renaissance."[6] He urged reaffirming ethical values in four areas to create this renaissance: stewardship, caring, accountability, and sharing. "Both business and government have to live within the tensions of accountability. Politicians cannot escape the process by claiming superior wisdom. Businesses cannot cite doctrines of free enterprise to escape accountability for their actions." Clearly the academic profession and higher education should likewise be held accountable. It has been too easy for academics to cite academic freedom and superior wisdom to avoid the responsibility of accountability.

Specifically related to higher education are the remarks of Dr. Donald Fredrickson, former director of the National Institute of Health. These comments are more broadly applicable than the health sciences of which he spoke. In speaking of the public patronage of science which grew so rapidly in the last quarter-century, he said:

> The purposes were simple. Information was to be discovered that could be transformed into better health and longer life for the investors and their children. The National Institutes of Health, assigned to sponsor the operation, became an almost unique example of government patronage and power to influence science. For nearly thirty-five years it has fostered self-governance by a profession that, because of the technical nature of the work, has borne responsibility for distributing public resources to itself. Performance of this trust has been uncompromising in its insistence on excellence and sound stewardship. And there is ample and continuing witness of our abundant return on the investment. Nevertheless, the past several years have been replete with signs—statements, editorials, actions—indicating that the relations between biomedical science and its public trustees are changing significantly, if not seriously decaying and in need of restoration. We are now in a major transitional phase. Under concerned public scrutiny, biomedical research is passing from an extended period of relative privacy and autonomy toward an engagement with new ethical, legal, and social imperatives. We move fitfully toward greater public governance of the sciences. For the sake of the public good, it is vital that we find the proper limits to this shift.[7]

The concluding remarks of Dr. Fredrickson are especially perti-
nent to all academics as we enter the last two decades of this
century.

> Some scientists will view the advent of more public gover-
> nance as evidence that science has passed through its Peri-
> clean Age and is in decline. I remind them of Toynbee's
> comments on the disintegration of the fountainhead of Hel-
> lenic society. The failure of Athens, he said, was one of lost
> initiative. In its dream of sovereignty, the elite and creative
> city ignored the political and economic dictates of the chang-
> ing civilization of which it was a part. The nemesis of creative
> institutions, Toynbee implies, is the temptation to idolize
> themselves to the point of failure to accommodate to altered
> realities. Thus, the isolation of Athens had to end, but its
> brilliance could have survived.

Can our academic creative institutions accommodate to the
altered realities? Have we idolized the academic profession to
such an extent that initiatives have been lost?

DOLLARS AND SCHOLARS

Our basic areas of interest and concern are outlined below and
developed in more detail in the following chapters. We believe
that ethical foundations are necessary for guiding the decisions
on the economics of the academic profession. Thus ethics comes
first. This is followed by two chapters on total faculty earnings
and sources of these earnings. The specific areas of continuing
education, intellectual properties and government support each
merit separate chapters. The concluding chapter provides a summary, conclusions and recommendations.

ETHICAL DILEMMAS

The teaching of ethics and values and their enforcement has
become a popular subject in recent years. The Hastings Center
is publishing a series of studies on the teaching of ethics in
undergraduate and graduate courses, and specific monographs on
the teaching of ethics in law, business, social sciences, engineering, journalism, bioethics, and public policy.[8] Ethics instruction
is becoming a well-developed field with many hundreds of programs encompassing most professional schools and many undergraduate curricula nationally. Seminars and symposia regarding
professional ethics are increasingly common. Under public pressure or by voters' mandate, legislative bodies have established
ethics committees, stricter guidelines, and rules for dozens of
professions.

While the professions, government, and business grope for viable rules of conduct, the academy—which frequently sends its members to guide others' deliberation—is oddly silent. Only a third of the graduate deans of research universities indicated in a recent survey that their institutions sponsored guest lecturers or colloquia dealing with ethical issues related to the academician's role; about the same number indicated that ethical issues were included as portions of other graduate courses. Only five institutions (out of 88 respondents) indicated one or more courses with a specific focus on professional ethics for academicians, and the survey indicated little interest in the future development of such courses. The academic interest in ethical issues is directed largely at other professions and not inward, toward the academic profession itself.[9]

Self-examination is overdue for those who so readily counsel others, for the unanswered questions are many. How do existing university rules and professional standards influence the objectives of academe? Do they support or compromise academic freedom and intellectual objectivity? Is conflict of interest (or even the appearance of conflict of interest) clearly defined and avoided? Do adequate policies exist? Are they enforced in a consistent and impartial manner? Too often in our studies we found negative answers to these questions. Existing policy and ethical standards are frequently inadequate and honored only in the breech.

FOR WHAT ARE FACULTY PAID? [10]

The "fulltime" faculty member is not required to work fulltime. Most faculty members in effect have but three-quarters time appointments, because they are employed for only nine months. For a three-month period each year, they can take other employment, or not, as they see fit. It is time belonging to the individual. Even during the academic year, formal teaching assignments normally do not exceed 12 student-contact hours per week for 30-32 weeks, and teaching loads frequently are less. Academics thus have the privilege of self-determination in the use of the great majority of their time—time which is considered to be paid for by their employers. Administrators assume their faculty will fill the balance of the work week in a manner beneficial to teaching, scholarship and service. (That benefit "repays" the salary and facilities investment by society.)

The fundamental problem is determining how much faculty commitment is due the employing institution for the base salary. Without that minimal standard, it is difficult for the institution to make a valid claim upon time faculty members consider to be their own, and equally difficult for faculty to establish valid claim to that time which they consider to be their own. The determination requires balancing these competing claims and presents an ethical problem involving a conflict of interest in how such time is spent, whether in additional institutional responsibilities or in outside income-producing labors. A second ethical issue flows from potential bias and loss of intellectual objectivity which can be introduced by supplemental income work.

Another set of economic issues relates to the institution. Base salary covers only some modest level of teaching, and additional teaching is compensated by overload salary. Salary above base is also paid by the institution for administration and, less frequently, for research, curriculum development, and other activities. Summer work for academic year faculty always is for additional compensation, since the summer is unpaid time belonging to the faculty member.

Professional and economic benefits from extra-institutional enterprises by faculty can be important, but the potential for ethical problems, in particular for conflicts of interest, is also considerable. University policy governing such matters as private professional practice or consulting, to name two common sources of income supplements, is frequently not comprehensive and very often is loosely administered.[11] Some alternative to the private, entrepreneurial nature of the present system, preferably one generated from within rather than imposed from without, might vest these economic benefits to the institutions, instead of to individual faculty members.

IMPLICATIONS FOR CONTINUING EDUCATION

Education of adults is a big and growing business, ranging from in-house training programs, to proprietary schools, and programs run by professional associations to university extensions and continuing education curricula. Many of the latter institutions have viewed expanding adult programs as a solution to declining enrollments of traditional undergraduate students. Here, too, lie many of the same ethical and economic issues submerged in the "regular" session. Many instructors in these programs are employed full-time as regular faculty and teach overload in adult or continuing education programs. Few institutions have any regular tenure track faculty in their continuing education programs. Some faculty members teach in continuing education for another institution whose programs may compete with the home institution, again clearly posing an ethical problem. Other faculty are involved in ownership of a continuing education company, in effect, competing with their "daylight" employer. Property rights for educational materials developed for adult education is an unsettled, problem-laden issue as well.

INTELLECTUAL PROPERTY

By tradition or by policy, most institutions permit faculty to have complete ownership of such intellectual property as textbooks or other copyrightable educational materials, computer software and creative arts. Patentable inventions resulting from university-paid employment (and use of university facilities) are usually owned by the institution, but royalty sharing is generous to the inventor(s), 35-50 percent being common. Large sums are at stake. On a national basis, textbook royalties may exceed $100 million annually for all college faculty.* Many faculty do consulting or are involved in their own businesses, usually in work related to their professional university work. These consulting and business activities may take from the university many potentially valuable intellectual properties. Yet it is probably not possible for a faculty member to create and profit from intellectual property in his professional field without drawing on university resources in some significant if indirect manner. With the electronic revolution and its potential for education and management, the university resources of libraries, computers, TV centers, word processing, and so on become both increasingly more important to faculty in the development of valuable intellectual property, and more costly to the university to develop and maintain. Yet all or a large share of the financial rewards flowing from intellectual property accrue to the individual faculty member, quite as if these facilities were fringe benefits to employment. This sanctioned appropriation suggests the need for different intellectual property management systems.

GOVERNMENT SUPPORT

Government support has become a large fiscal element in the overall budgets of all major research universities. With few exceptions, even institutions whose primary function is teaching rely on government for some support. Grant and contract support is usually project-oriented, provides summer salary for faculty on academic year appointments, and may pay all or part of academic

---

*Estimate made by Robert H. Linnell.

year salary. The ethical questions, not to mention the financial, are considerable, not the least when academic interests are directed toward areas where funding is available. Sub-disciplines, specialties, even whole departments grow up, flourish or die with the financial nurturing or lack of it from extra-university funding sources. The impact on free academic inquiry is clear, on curricula clearer still. Colleges and universities must have resources from society in order to operate. Funds from government are important but we must seek funding mechanisms that will not destroy the very freedom which has made it possible for academe to play its unique role in society.

THE FUTURE

All these issues, and more, must be weighed in a time when social institutions and the professions generally are being subjected to closer public scrutiny and regulation. Higher education will be held accountable no more, but no less, than government and private industry. Colleges and universities must compete for resources along with a long list of others—all of whom can plead special value to their cause. Academic freedom is as unacceptable as a basis for unsatisfactory (and unenforced) ethical standards for the academic profession as is the doctrine of free enterprise an unacceptable excuse for unethical business behavior. Thus it is essential for the academy to come to grips with these issues, creating and enforcing ethical standards that will merit the support of society. In return, society must provide the resources necessary for higher education to serve the important role needed in the emerging information, post-industrial world.

References

1 *The Financial Status of the Professor in America and in Germany*, Bulletin No. 2, p. VII, Carnegie Foundation for the Advancement of Teaching, New York, May 1908.

2 Hansen, W.L. *Academic Compensation: Myths and Realities.* Fourth Annual Planning Conference, University of Southern California, Office of Institutional Studies, Los Angeles, CA 90089. June 11-13, 1979.

3 Dunham, R.E., Wright, P.S. and Chandler, M.O. *Teaching Faculty in Universities and Four Year Colleges.* U.S. Office of Education, Washington, D.C. 1966.

4 Marsh, H.W. *Total Faculty Earnings, Academic Productivity and Demographic Variables. Fourth Annual Academic Planning Conference,* University of Southern California, Office of Institutional Studies, Los Angeles, CA 90089. June 11-12, 1979. A shorter version has been published, Marsh, H.W. and Dillon, K.E. "Academic Productivity and Faculty Supplemental Income," *Journal of Higher Education,* 51 (No. 5, 1980): 546-555.

5 *Fair Practices in Higher Education: Rights and Responsibilites of Students and their Colleges in a Period of Intensified Competition for Enrollment.* A Report of the Carnegie Council on Policy Studies in Higher Education. Jossey-Bass Publishers, San Francisco (1979).

6 The Second National Conference on Business Ethics, Bentley College, Waltham, Mass. 02154. April 7-8, 1978.

7 Fredrickson, Donald S. "The Public Governance of Science," Columbia University Bicentennial Lecture, December 9, 1976. Published in *Man and Medicine,* Vol. 3, No. 2, 1978.

8 Institute of Society, Ethics and Life Sciences, The Hastings Center, 360 Broadway, Hastings-on-Hudson, New York 10706. Publication series on the teaching of ethics in higher education.

9 Dillon, Kristine E. *University Policy Survey.* An unpublished report on 168 Research and Doctorate Granting Universities, (88 Respondents). Office of Institutional Studies, University of Southern California, Los Angeles, CA 90089. The entire May/June 1982 issue of *The Journal of Higher Education* (Vol. 53, No. 3) has the title, Ethics and the Academic Profession.

10 Dillon, K.E., and Linnell, Robert H., *How and for What are Professors Paid?* National Forum Vol. LX, No. 2, Spring 1980. pp. 21-23.

11 Dillon, Kristine E., and Bane, Karen L., "Analysis of University Policies for Consulting and Conflict-of-Interest," *Educational Record,* Spring, 1980, pp. 55-72.

2. The Ethics of the Academic Profession

Henry B. Clark and Kristine E. Dillon

ETHICS, EVEN IN A PLURALISTIC, secular culture, is a normative concept. It deals with principles of right and wrong, good and evil, in a manner which transcends taste, manners, mores, prudence and even legality. Ethical norms govern the network of mutual relationships that individuals have with each other and with the institutions to which they belong. Ethical ideals elicit and reinforce concern for one's fellow citizens and service to them beyond the realm of obligations defined by law and custom. Ethics, and the definitions of ethical behavior, are changeable. As society evolves, the specific behavioral implications of ethical norms and ideals are redefined to some extent by succeeding generations. No major social institution or profession is immune to this reflection and redefinition, including the Academy. It is of particular importance today for colleges and universities, their faculties, their students, and the society which supports them to examine academic ethical standards and clarify what is to be expected and encouraged (and by implication, that which is to be discouraged). The issues to be explored are significant and of concern to all academic professionals.

Ethical questions are not properly decided by the relative power of competing interest groups. With respect to the academy, a professor's wishes for security vis-a-vis his or her employer, popularity vis-a-vis students, or prestige in the eyes of professional colleagues are not adequate ethical reasons for doing or not doing anything. Nor is an inadequate salary an ethical basis for engaging in outside business ventures or other extra income generating activities. Indeed, honest ethical analysis tries to bracket such considerations so that they will not unduly influence the search for the right course of action. Although it may be tempting, the reduction of ethical dilemmas to problems that can be solved by reference to political clout, economic rationality, or administrative finesse evades the substance of ethics. Furthermore, such solutions often do not adequately satisfy the concerns which created the problem.

Many public observers would probably define ethics for the academic profession primarily in terms of such individual virtues as reliability, honesty, and objectivity. Integrity in a scholar or teacher is often thought to consist of competence, diligence, and seriousness of purpose in the pursuit of truth; thus plagiarism or falsification of data are virtually unforgivable sins. To some extent behavior of this kind can be dealt with in a professional association's code of ethics since it is used to promote high standards of behavior. Ethicists feel, however, that such a code of ethics will be only of limited effectiveness unless it is adopted in spirit as well as in letter.[1] Ethical responsibility in the fullest sense within the professoriate requires adoption of an integrated mechanism of accountability which draws, in appropriate degrees, upon three types of regulators of professional conduct: contract, code, and covenant.[2]

Contracts emphasize clearly understood, generally written stipulations of rights and duties agreed upon by employer and employee and if violations occur, subject to legal sanctions. Many of the ethical dilemmas arising today in academe could be clarified or resolved by more clearly designed contractual agreements.

Professional *codes* of ethics require high performance standards of professionals, but if the ethos of the professional association is guild-oriented (as is frequently true), the code as an operative force may consist primarily of rules and admonitions designed to maintain order and respectability. This may have little effect save that of attempting to ensure the profession high status.

The concept of a *covenant* between a professional and his clients and colleagues refers to a definition of behavior which transcends those included in the contract or code. Operating within a covenant, the professional's understanding of his individual responsibilities and the collective responsibilities of the profession goes beyond anything stipulated by contract or motivated by self-interest. In this sense, covenant is used to describe a bond linking persons in the same social or political community where due recognition is made of the interdependence of all individuals and of the reciprocal obligations they have toward each other as a result of this interdependence. As contrasted with code or contract, it transcends minimalism or legalism in the definition of the rights and responsibilities of the group of persons concerned. It provides a guide to individual behavior that goes beyond self-interest, and, in the ultimate, to that of society as a whole.

To apply these concepts to concrete examples, consider Professor Brown who, because of a consultancy for a firm which pays a good fee for his services, fails to meet eight of his thirty classes during a fifteen-week semester and is never present at the meetings of two committees to which he has been assigned. Such behavior is obviously unethical and unprofessional in a very basic sense, and rules to define and discourage it (regarding both work and time obligations), can be spelled out in faculty contracts. Proper conduct in this respect can also be covered in a code of academic ethics elaborated by a professional guild and used by it to discipline the membership. The same is true of materials and equipment issues: the use of university materials and/or facilities such as specialized laboratory equipment or computers which results in the earning of external income can be regulated by guild standards and by specific contract agreements.

But what about the problems raised in the more elusive ethical areas such as objectivity? Professor Smith meets all of the classes, does all her committee work faithfully and continues to publish a respectable number of articles irreproachable in quality of scholarly methodology but limited entirely to the interests of her consulting clientele. Her research has become so narrowly focused that she has lost the ability to step back and ask, "What *are* the important issues in my field?" It would be very difficult to fault such a person on legal or professional grounds unless a conception of responsibilities larger than those spelled out in a contract or code were allowed to come into play. Yet this individual might be guilty of violating the highest ideals of the vocation, especially if the objectivity which is a crucial aspect of integrity is conceived of as demanding reasonable comprehensiveness in data collection, agenda-setting, and research behavior.

Beyond contract and code lies a covenant with the ultimate client, namely, one's *profession* and one's *institution* or, more broadly, society as a whole. One of the benefits of this covenant is that it serves as a reminder of a responsibility to do more than exercise a personal calling with skill and compassion, but to see to it that the entire institution—the schools, departments and disciplines—keeps convenant with those whom it serves and who provide it support. This concept significantly broadens accountability beyond that of personal agency. The crucial difference between the letter (rules, contractual agreements) and the spirit (convenantal ideal) of a code of ethics is that the former is oriented toward *administrative clarity* whereas the latter is concerned with *outcomes*—i.e., outcomes which do justice to all elements of the client-system.

Even without formal statement, the covenantal commitment is pivotal. A contract may obligate a faculty member to serve on three departmental or university committees each year if asked to do so. But only a covenantal understanding of duty to do one's share of the housekeeping chores of the institution is likely to elicit the fullest and best contribution to the work of these committees; otherwise, the faculty member may turn out to be a surly obstructionist or a spineless wielder of the rubber stamp (simply because the meetings will end sooner if nobody raises any questions about anything).

Similarly, a contract may oblige a researcher to share the proceeds of his endeavors (including the royalties and the patent rights or copyrights) with the university and the colleagues without whose help the achievement in question could not have been realized. But unless the principal agent in such enterprises is morally convinced (as he would be with the covenant concept) of the justice of sharing rewards, he may be evasive, niggardly or downright dishonest in seeking to keep these returns for himself. No contract is apt to suffice when it comes to a professional's duties to the "ultimate client," that is, society as a whole (or even the profession as a whole). Even a code by itself cannot suffice in this regard. But a scholar/teacher who is committed to a covenant concept of his professional obligations is not likely to be satisfied with mere administrative guidelines in his selection of research agenda, his methods of analysis, his teaching, or what he does with his findings and the impact they have on the field or, ultimately, on society.*

---

*It means, for example, that the scientist who develops new strains of high yield wheat which become a part of the "Green Revolution" and the engineer who seeks to invent new farm machinery must look beyond the laboratory and assess the impact of their discoveries as they are used in the food production system. If their research results in even higher rates of pollution because of the heavy use of chemical fertilizers required by the new type of grain, and in even greater concentration of land ownership and less food for poor people because of the high cost of the machinery and its use on cash crops for export instead of food crops for citizens of third world nations, they cannot be satisfied with their work. They may want to start looking for a different variety of wheat and for

Most long-time inhabitants of academe would freely acknowledge that these practices are not particularly unusual. Indeed, many observers would declare that what is unusual is the flurry of concern about the propriety of such practices which has arisen in recent years. However, it is clear that all major institutions of our society today are being pressed with the claims of social accountability—and this means that many heretofore accepted patterns of action of professors (as well as corporation executives and government officials) are being subjected to scrutiny and, frequently, demands for change.

The picture is complicated further by the fact that accountability claims are being advanced from many different quarters. Professional persons, in particular, are being bombarded by demands from a variety of "client-systems," each of which cries, "You must be more accountable to *me!*" and sets forth a slightly different bill of particulars. Academic professionals receive mixed, and sometimes conflicting, signals from their employers, their students, their professional colleagues, and society as a whole.

The external pressure manifested in the "raised accountability consciousness" of the various clients of academic professionals, and the newly insistent claims being registered because of it, may

---

more appropriate agricultural technology, and they may want to look for other patrons who will use their inventions more carefully and put them to better use. (L.A. Times, April 20, 1979) Above all, they will be sensitive to the conflicts-of-interest involved in situations such as the one attacked in a recent law suit filed by the California Rural Legal Assistance. The suit "charges that the University of California's research program . . . is for sale, cheap, to large agribusiness concerns." By investing 5 percent of the cost of a given project, "donors" can dictate how the full 100 percent of total funds (where the remaining 95 percent come from state and federal funds) are used. The suit also contends that: UC professors, who have enormous discretion over their own research programs, are allowed to work on public time in UC laboratories and with UC equipment on projects from which they personally will receive large profits. For example, one faculty member, who receives an annual salary of $40,500, has collected more than $250,000 in royalties for agricultural machines that he developed with public funds. The lawsuit is not intended "to halt mechanization, technology, or 'progress'," nor does it attempt "to stop the development of every machine." But agricultural research that abandons the interests of farm workers, small farmers and consumers is not progress, "and it is intended to challenge such one-sided research" and to question "the type of machines that are developed, and how these decisions are made, and who is being helped or hurt by particular machines." Clearly, faculty engaged in such activities should also deal with ethical issues such as these as part of their professional responsibilities.

be related to a decline in what may once have been a more commonly understood and accepted idea of professional ethics. According to William Van Alstyne, this may be due to greater diversity within the professoriate:

> With the immense growth of higher education since World War II . . . , those drawn into university teaching and administration may well have less in common than one supposes—and correspondingly, may have less in common as to what they suppose a good academic common law contains.[3]

Whether or not this "decline" has occurred, there are those who believe that complete self-regulation is not a realistic function for the academic profession—or any other profession—to assume.[4] Academics are more likely than other professionals to be confronted with conflicts of obligation than with conflicts of interest, William F. May has observed. The difficulty encountered by today's academician lies in successfully allocating appropriate amounts of energy and time among the numerous areas of faculty responsibility comprising "teaching, research, and public service."[5] Complete self-regulation may not be feasible, but it does seem reasonable to expect faculty to assess responsibly the growing range of services expected of them, rethink priorities for the application of their expertise, and after doing so, clearly communicate the standards they adopt to their clients and the general public.

At a 1977 conference on academic ethics at the University of Southern California, one of the speakers noted:

> Not long ago, the average citizen regarded the universities and their faculties as being on a higher plane than most other segments of our society. They were considered to be ethical, scholarly, interested in learning and knowledge and truth for their own sakes and thus different from other sectors of society which were regarded as mundane and self-seeking. In more recent times, however, our universities and many of their faculty members have begun to resemble other pressure groups . . . seeking more grants and more money, more perquisites, and sometimes being quite arrogant about it. When this is coupled with possible conflicts of interest, self-enrichment, sometimes dubious or unseemly practices or outright abuse of the system, how can we expect to remain on the high pedestal where we once stood? To my mind this represents a great loss for an institution which for a very long time has been considered one of the most honorable and highly regarded pillars of our civilization . . . .[6]

Academics are forewarned. The public rejects the idea than any select elite is immune to accountability and those who attempt to obtain exemption are, ironically, most likely to receive critical assessment. The strongest stance higher education can take against external regulation is that of responsible internal evaluation and modification where necessary. The most certain way to have complex ethical issues resolved by an insensitive external agent is, as Stephen Bailey noted, "to pretend that we are free from sin and that in any case government has no right to invade our bastions of sacred immunity even when we are unjust."[7]

We are not free of sin, nor the appearance of sin. Crucial questions center on faculty work time and who owns it, the use of university materials and equipment, and the use of university personnel—especially secretaries and students. Is time due the university and/or students misspent when a faculty member holds a consultancy? Would the donation of a certain percentage of the income (proportionate to the percentage of time invested by university personnel during the normal workday) restore the moral balance? For example, in the case where the faculty member develops a textbook with the aid of bibliographies prepared by graduate students, typing by university clerical staff, and the use of library and office facilities, is there anything wrong about the faculty member's receiving all of the royalties from sales of the book? Is it improper for the book to be a required text in the author's course? Is it more ethical for the author to receive no royalties from on-campus sales of the text? If so, is it something that should be contractually *required* of everyone, or expected (but not required) of everyone, or simply admired in those who choose to act in this fashion?

Similar to this case is the one where works of art are created using university materials and equipment. Typically, the faculty artist receives all proceeds of any sales. Is the reflected prestige that the university may gain from a successful artist (or performing musician) sufficient to warrant this arrangement? Or does university support actually serve as an incentive to engage in the independent marketing of creative works—perhaps to the detriment of other university duties?

A somewhat different situation is that where faculty (or academic administrators) are significantly involved in outside, professionally related business ventures. In addition to the potential conflict of interest in work time (and who owns it) and commitment to institutional purposes there is a very complex problem in separation of academic interests from business interests. It is doubtful if this latter separation can be achieved and therefore there must inevitably be some loss in that freedom of work which is so cherished and basic to the academic enterprise.

In this period of burgeoning (and often competing) programs of continuing education, what should the university policy be regarding teaching in another institution's continuing education program *if this competes* with programs offered at the "home" institution? How should the university and the academic profession react to the faculty member who teaches for private business or industry or within a professional association's continuing education program rather than for his or her own university? Does it make a difference if the external program competes with an existing university program or not? Perhaps the university would like to plan a new continuing education program but is preempted by an existing program taught by a university faculty member.*

Other problems occur in situations where a conflict of interest is likely. Here the fundamental question is that of objectivity: can any person, even a learned scholar or highly trained technical expert, who may stand to profit by defending a certain body of facts or ideas preserve the impartiality of his judgment in a situation where he is asked to evaluate that body of knowledge vis-a-vis contrary facts, opinions, analyses, interpretations and policy recommendations? Is it unethical for him to be biased, that is, does integrity necessarily require impartiality? Or is it simply unethical not to disclose his potential conflict of interest?

In another instance, conflict of interest can arise when, as is increasingly the case, a faculty member who has applied for grant support is told that funding will be offered at a lower level and that adjustments to the proposed budget must be made to reflect the cut. All too often, the faculty member is placed in the situation of responsibility for a budget modification that will have direct financial impact on him and his university. In the instance where a portion of the faculty member's salary during the academic year as well as summer salary are in the original budget, it is clearly tempting to delete the grant contribution to academic year salary since it must be paid by the university anyway. Here again, the faculty member is trying to serve multiple clients and some alternatives with which he is faced carry personal economic benefits, the choice of which may mark him as being self-serving at university or public expense. This type of problem could, in principle, be solved by bureaucratic rules—a solution which most faculty would dislike and which might also reduce the effective-

---

*Survey responses from 125 deans and directors of Continuing Education indicated that almost 60 percent felt that their institution should prohibit regular faculty from "moonlighting teaching" if it was in competition with programs offered by their own school of continuing education (See page 74, Chapter 5).

ness of research funding. The choice may therefore be one of
individual ethics vs. management responsibility.

In order to deal with such ethical concerns as those raised above, faculty and their universities must be, first of all, conscious that such practices warrant their attention and, second, willing to discuss such issues on a recurrent basis so that a community sense of appropriate behavior is developed and understood. Such discussions will probably result in modifications in some existing university policies and/or practices regarding consulting, outside businesses, intellectual property rights, overload and outside teaching, and grant management. Such changes would doubtlessly reflect the heightened sensitivity academic professionals would develop as a result of their own discussions and the increased societal and university attention paid to these issues.

Some institutions now have an array of policies and practices which reflect the mix of covenant, code, and contract appropriate to their own unique situations. These institutions could be described as having contractual codes for faculty which encourage and reinforce a covenantal sense of ethical responsibility. Combined with the regular opportunity for faculty and administration to participate in self and institutional assessment concerning the ethics of the academic profession, such efforts at self-regulation can serve as indication of academe's response to the need for accountability. This is greatly needed.

Some of the more comprehensive and carefully designed policies now followed by universities establish accountability over a wide spectrum of concerns, ranging from use of university-funded time, facilities, and personnel to conflicts of interest and influence peddling. Behavior in conformity with the guidelines established on these matters is usually mandatory, and faculty members must operate at all times in accordance with the principles of full disclosure and advance consultation with the department head or appropriate dean. Communications concerning outside commitments are in writing, and an annual written report confirming compliance with the regulation governing the total number of days devoted to consulting in a given contract period is also required. This means that a faculty member's observance of the guidelines is a matter of record and can be checked and used as a basis for enforcing sanctions if noncompliance is revealed at some later date.

The complement of careful policy-making must be the encouragement of professional self-regulation on an individual basis. The integrated mechanism of fostering ethical behavior within the profession seems to lie in the reciprocal relationship of university rules and the integrity of the faculty itself. And the judgment of individual faculty members will always be an important factor. Most academicians feel strongly that the kind of autonomy important to intellectual and creative pursuits cannot be maintained if measures of accountability are based only upon detailed and numerous regulations. However, independence from restricting regulations will clearly require a clearer demonstration of responsible peer- and self-regulation based upon conscious awareness of ethical issues.

Mutual accountability of faculty and their university is an essential feature of any workable mechanism of accountability. Therefore, the development of an appropriate mechanism must stem from the following premises: 1) bureaucratic organizations can easily become antithetical to the academic role, but 2) bureaucracy is inescapable in the management of a large, complex, modern university, and therefore, 3) the problem to be solved is the development of organizational structures and a definition of roles and role relationships which achieve an optimal balance between the need for autonomy and the need for accountability.

Acknowledgement of the preceding view of the university leads to the following recommendations:

Sound academic ethics require that more attention be given to the specification of contractual obligations between faculty members and the universities which employ them. Clear policies should be spelled out in the written agreements entered into by both parties. The policy handbook should specify how adherence to policies will be monitored, the processes to be followed, and penalties when violation of policy is established.

An academic code of ethics is an essential component of the mechanism that promotes ethical behavior. Though such codes are insufficient to assure the deeper professional commitment of the academicians, they do have value as symbolic points of reference. The real value of such codes lies in the process of bringing minds into mutual understanding, whereas the outward and mechanical coordination of such changes may be less effective alone. For this reason, it is desirable for a code of academic ethics to be hammered out with extensive faculty participation. A code written by the administration, a professional association, or a small group of faculty representatives, and then imposed cannot have nearly the effect upon increasing the awareness of all members of the faculty that wider participation would have. The time-consuming process required to develop a code which reflects a consensus among the faculty and administration, while admittedly not an efficient use of time from a policy-maker's viewpoint, is likely to be the most effective way to guarantee the acceptance and observance of the code's intent.

Much greater attention to peer review of internal and external conduct by the faculty is required. Having labored through the preparation of a code of ethics, the institution must establish machinery and procedures for systematically reviewing the professional conduct of faculty members, both in their activities within the university and in their professional activities beyond its walls. A code alone easily becomes lip service to a set of ideals no one takes seriously. The interests of the profession must be maintained and reinforced repeatedly to counteract the individual interests which are always present. Preservation of academic professionalism calls not only for a defense of academic freedom and autonomy, but for effective self-regulation of conduct as well. Credibility of peer review can probably be established only by some involvement of qualified but disinterested individuals from outside the institution, some of whom will not be academicians. Failure of institutions to establish such review mechanisms may lead to their imposition by outside agencies. Furthermore, serious transgression of the code of ethics must be dealt with strongly and forthrightly; otherwise, the integrity of the entire process will be compromised and it will be of little value.

Mutual public disclosure of income and time allocations is an essential means of achieving mutual accountablility of faculty members and their universities. The reciprocity re-enforces the covenant among academicians, universities, and the public, while demonstrating a non-hierarchical relationship with respect to accountability among these three groups. Openness regarding these matters supports the argument that uses of professional time and institutional resources result in worthy and important contributions to society by the academic community.

Finally, it appears that increased awareness of ethical issues confronting the academic profession could be achieved effectively through the inclusion of formal coursework in academic ethics in the graduate programs of those seeking the doctorate and planning on an academic career. Exclusive emphasis on scholarly expertise does not provide complete preparation for a position that involves as many teaching and administrative responsibilities as the typical faculty job entails or for a career in which ethical sensitivity is so essential.

In the coming years, it seems clear that professional demands for autonomy and public demands for consumer protection and cost effectiveness will tug at opposite ends of society's "rope." If higher education is able to demonstrate that it can responsibly monitor and account for the behavior of academic professionals, perhaps some of that tension will be avoided. Higher education's recognition of society's priorities and definitions of acceptable ranges of behavior can serve to justify in return the opportunity to determine how best to provide an environment conducive to creative intellectual exploration and scholarship. Only through such a balance can the goals of both society and higher education be met.

References

1 Callahan, D. "Should There Be An Academic Code of Ethics?" Presented at the 1979 National Conference on Higher Education of the American Association for Higher Education (AAHE), Washington, D.C., April 1979. See also, under the same title and author, *Journal of Higher Education L III* No.3, pp. 335-344 (1982).

2 May, W.F. "Code, Covenant, Contract, or Philanthropy." *Hastings Center Report 5* (December 1975) 29-38.

3 Van Alstyne, W. "Faculty Codes and Professional Responsibility." In *The Ethics of Teaching and Scientific Research*, pp. 83-86. Edited by Hook, et al. New York: Prometheus Books, 1977.

4 Bailey, S.K. "The Peculiar Mixture: Public Norms and Private Space." In *Government Regulation of Higher Education*, pp. 103-112. Edited by W.C. Hobbs, Cambridge, Massachusetts: Ballinger Pub. Co., 1978.

5 May, W.F. "Academic Expertise and Service to Society." Presented at the Fourth Annual Academic Planning Conference, University of Southern California, Los Angeles, June 1979.

6 Levin, L. "Salary Reimbursement—Benefits and Costs." Presented at the Second Annual Academic Planning Conference, University of Southern California, Los Angeles, January 1977.

7 Bailey, op. cit.

3. Economics of the Academic Profession: A Perspective on Total Professional Earnings

Kristine E. Dillon

THE TREMENDOUS GROWTH in higher education in the 1950s and 1960s created both an unprecedented increase in faculty positions and a market that encouraged the production of large numbers of qualified would-be academics. Given the increasingly austere view for higher education, it is not clear how the expectations engendered during that period can be fulfilled or satisfactorily modified.

Twenty years ago, competition for relatively scarce faculty resulted in higher salaries, better fringe benefits, and more attractive working conditions; in the 1980s the university appears to offer fewer opportunities, let alone enticements, to the prospective (or incumbent) academician. Faculty salaries during the 1950s and 1960s outpaced the cost of living by about 65 percent, but fell behind in the next decade.[1] Moreover, as the decade of the seventies came to a close, a noticeable divergence emerged between faculty salaries and the Consumer Price Index (CPI).[2,3] While it is premature to anticipate a reversal of this trend, it is true that for the first time since 1976, faculty salaries increased relative to the CPI both in 1980-81 and 1981-82.[4] These two years' increases resulted in a modest improvement in faculty purchasing power. Furthermore the many nonmonetary returns from academic employment should not be discounted or overlooked. However, even after acknowledging such intangibles as status and freedom of intellectual pursuit, many faculty are still frustrated today by a perceived weakening in their economic situation.

When salaries are examined in light of stabilizing enrollments and the surplus of qualified faculty, it appears that . . ."The basic trend in faculty salaries has been more closely linked to public attitudes about the value of higher education than to market demand. . . ."[5] Howard R. Bowen cites recent high rates of inflation as probably the most responsible for the slipping level of faculty salaries, but some public disenchantment with the value of a college education is also having its effect.

Given this assessment, analyses of faculty compensation must examine not only current patterns and sources of earnings but also their potential effects on public perceptions of these patterns and sources . . . and, even more sobering, their impact upon the quality of higher education itself. If, for instance, the opportunity for faculty in many disciplines to obtain consultancies has helped to ease higher education's concern about low salaries, what impact do such practices have on higher education's ability to justify requests for increased funding for faculty salaries?

There is evidence of legislative concern about activities that supplement faculty income or involve time that appears already to be salaried and thus belongs to the institution. Increased governmental attention to time accountability, reflected in such university requirements as "monitored workloads" and "personnel activity reports" for funded research projects, reflects suspicion that outside activities drain off significant amounts of faculty time. It may be that this time should be devoted to research projects for which faculty are paid out of public monies. In the past, it was generally assumed that faculty time was devoted primarily to university responsibilities including funded research; this assumption is now being seriously questioned.

While some faculty consulting activities have aroused concern, most university administrators, faculty, students, and external users acknowledge that consulting can be beneficial both to educational institutions and to those who retain the teacher-as-consultant. But questions remain whether, in serving as a professional for hire, the faculty member is motivated primarily by entrepreneurial rather than by intellectual interests.

Funded summer research and consulting are not the only major
sources of supplemental professional income, since many faculty
regularly draw supplemental earnings from royalties, lecture and
speech fees, and diverse other activities. Summer and overload
teaching are in fact the two major sources of extra income for
faculty members.*

All of these sources of earnings contribute to total professional
compensation. Their various impacts on faculty morale and institutional loyalty as well as their impacts on public perceptions of
higher education are increasingly important to an academy confronted with financial stringency. If, as Bowen believes, salary
levels are linked with public attitudes, institutional salaries may
continue to lag if public attitudes about higher education are
negatively influenced by *perceptions* of faculty behavior.

COMPARING FACULTY CHARACTERISTICS WITH THOSE OF OTHER WORKERS

The faculty role is generally acknowledged as unique among
forms of employment. The unusual, even extraordinary, work
characteristics are paralleled by the ways in which faculty members receive compensation. Perceived as "professionals" (the label
signifying one who has an assured competence in a field or
occupation and who engages in that occupation for his or her
livelihood), faculty members do not fit neatly into any of the
usual categories of professional workers described below.

Fee-for-Service Professionals: This group is made up of persons
who charge clients for their services. Their work is in a sense
entrepreneurial since their economic well-being depends on their
own abilities to attract clients. Their work schedules, fees, and
any products derived from their professional expertise are self-
controlled, though influenced to some extent by what the market
(their clients) will bear.

Artists, Entertainers, and other Creative Professionals: While
similar to fee-for-service professionals, members of this group may
receive not only a flat fee for services or products but also
royalties or residuals derived from sales or recurring use of the
results of their work. This difference is most obviously accounted
for by the lack of job security afforded by the short-term nature of
their paid work activities. They rely on the marketplace and the
quality and success of their works for economic viability.

---

* Detailed data on sources of supplemental income are given in Chapter 4.

Salaried Professional Employees: Employed by industry, government, health, education, and nonprofit organizations, these professionals work regular hours but also work overtime with no additional compensation. This group is characterized by competitive salaries and benefits, and relatively secure positions. Since they are paid for their professional talents, they generally have limited or no rights to intellectual property created as a result of their professional expertise and employment. However, some employers provide profit-sharing opportunities or bonuses for especially valuable work by professional employees.

While not "professional," the *blue collar or skilled tradesman* category is important in the consideration of faculty work characteristics and compensation patterns. The members of this large group are generally paid by the hour for specific duties. Hours worked beyond the prescribed full-time workweek are compensated at an increased hourly rate. Pay is linked with measurable output since the assumption is made that each additional hour worked may be equated with some increase in output. Job security relies upon union contracts and seniority systems. Typically, union scale wages and fringe benefits are good and may even exceed salaries of professional workers.

In comparison with these various categories of workers, the academic professional has unusual employment characteristics. Most faculty members have the unique combination of a full-time salary for nine months (about 25 percent hold 12-month contracts); their scheduled work hours are 25 percent to 50 percent of the scheduled work hours of salaried professionals; and they have significant job security afforded through tenure. Characteristics of the fee-for-service and creative professionals are also found in the academic realm in the form of consulting and professional service fees and right to intellectual property. An element shared with workers in skilled trades is the opportunity to receive overload or override payments, similar to the tradesman's overtime. Faculty overload, however, appears to have one different characteristic, since it is usually at the same or a *lower* rate than their full-time rates while the tradesman's overtime is paid at a *higher* rate.

The faculty member appears to fare well in this comparison, except when the nine-month feature of guaranteed salary is examined more closely. Faculty who work only nine months a year may technically be considered part-time employees, with an assumption that their salaries are not intended to provide total annual earnings. Because of this factor and salaries lagging behind the pace of inflation, most faculty members do not depend exclusively on basic institutional salaries for their total earnings.

Traditionally, academic employment has been characterized by a very vague definition of a full-time faculty workload; hence the determination of "overload" is subject to debate. Faculty members are acknowledged to work long hours—well over 40 hours a week. Yet other professionals report comparable workweeks and, for most in the "salaried professional" category, these extra hours do not result in additional salary. Not so the academician. In addition to time off for consulting or other outside work, the faculty member can earn additional salary during the academic year within his or her institution and has summers free to earn extra compensation at the institution or elsewhere. Furthermore, in contrast to industry, such intellectual property rights as copyrights and works of art generally belong to faculty members; royalties from inventions resulting from research done at university expense are usually shared rather generously with faculty inventors by the university (i.e., frequently 35-50 percent of net royalties). Activities resulting in additional faculty earnings are widespread; 90 percent of nine-month faculty at four-year institutions earn some supplemental income.[6] Fall 1980 survey data on 1979-80 total faculty earnings indicated that 81 percent of all four-year college faculty with full-time, 9/10 month appointments, earn an average of 22 percent above base salary, excluding royalty income.[7] A similar survey in fall 1981 provides additional total earnings data for 1980-81: at Ph.D.-Granting Universities, 82.4 percent of all full-time faculty on academic year appointments reported an average of 29.4 percent above base earnings, including royalties; at institutions granting graduate degrees but not the Ph.D., 82.5 percent of the faculty averaged earnings above base of 22.2 percent; for institutions granting only bachelors degrees the corresponding figures were 80.9 percent of the faculty averaging 22.6 percent above base earnings.[8]

The sums involved in supplemental faculty salary are huge. By any assessment the economic viability of the academic profession needs to consider total faculty earnings and the sources from which these are derived. To what extent have academic professionals become dependent upon earnings from other than their base (contract) salaries for an adequate professional income? What is the impact on instructional programs, on scholarship and academic freedom, and on public service?

ALTERNATIVES TO TRADITIONAL SALARY STUDIES

Faculty compensation has been examined from a variety of perspectives. Most typically, data examined are those collected by the Association of American University Professors (AAUP) in conjunction with the National Center for Education Statistics (NCES). These data reflect each institution's average tenure track base salaries by rank and report all salaries on a 9-month basis, converting any 12-month earnings to their proportional 9-month amounts. Thus, the standard basis for assessing academic earnings intentionally *excludes* all summer and overload or override salaries paid by institutions and clearly *does not* include any non-university earnings.

In a comprehensive assessment of the status of academic compensation, Howard R. Bowen noted that data collection regarding salaries has traditionally been undertaken for the primary purpose of inter-institutional comparisons.[9] As the whole of higher education finds itself in a depressed economic state, attempts have been made to use these traditionally-collected salary data to make comparisons with the earnings of those working outside academe. At this point 9-month contract salary and compensation data become inadequate since the comparison earnings for non-academic professionals are derived from 12-month employment. To make accurate comparisons with the earnings of other professionals, comprehensive data which account for faculty earnings from all professional sources and/or for full 12-month employment are needed.

Higher education does not routinely collect such information but rather maintains salary data in the format specified by the AAUP/NCES. Still a number of other salary compensation data bases are available, each with its own limitations, but presenting a more comprehensive perspective on total academic earnings than that provided by 9-month contract salary data. These "alternative" salary data indicate that, when total professional earnings are considered, faculty earnings are not necessarily in the serious state of decline many fear. More importantly, however, faculty increasingly depend upon a diversity of funding sources (employers) for their professional incomes.

When comparisons with nonacademic 12-month earnings rely upon 9-month academic earnings, it is clear that academicians are usually not competitive with outside professionals. However, since total faculty earnings are usually considerably higher than 9-month salaries, they compare more favorably than is generally reported. In a comparison based upon data from the U.S. Bureau of the Census "Current Population Survey" for 1977, faculty were centered close to average earnings for 16 groups of individuals with jobs classified as professional or management who had completed six or more years of college and worked at least 35 hours a week for a minimun of 40 weeks during 1976 (table 1). While the professions of medicine and law raise the overall group mean, the

TABLE 1

MEAN PERSONAL EARNINGS IN 1976
RANKED BY OCCUPATION

	Occupation	Mean	Number
1.	Health Practitioners	$36,187	318
2.	Lawyers and Judges	28,175	234
3.	Managers and Executives	24,718	335
4.	Engineers	24,332	134
5.	Accountants	21,713	39
6.	University and School Administrators	21,378	161
7.	Scientists	21,054	72
8.	College Faculty	19,840	237
9.	Social Scientists	19,030	59
10.	Technicians	18,896	63
11.	Social and Recreation Workers, Counselors	15,750	96
12.	School Teachers	14,982	427
13.	Librarians and Curators	14,277	35
14.	Artists and Entertainers	13,995	47
15.	Health Workers	13,634	46
16.	Clergy and Religious	10,418	101

	Mean	Number	Median
College Faculty	$19,840	237	$18,286
TOTAL GROUP	22,133	2,404	18,612

Source: Dillon, Kristine E., and Marsh, Herbert W., "Faculty Earnings Compared with Those of Nonacademic Professionals" *Journal of Higher Education, 52* (No. 6, 1981): 615-623.

median (or midpoint earnings figure) for the total group is very close to the median for college faculty. These census data, though limited to a very general form of earnings comparison, suggest that total faculty earnings are not significantly out of keeping with those of other professionals, despite the fact that 9-month faculty salaries look very low when compared with earnings outside academe.[10]

Like many other workers, academicians have felt they experienced serious economic setbacks in the face of a rapidly rising CPI. The American people in general secured wage gains less than inflationary increases during the peak of double digit inflation. The private non-farm sector experienced an average wage gain in 1979 of 8.7 percent, compared with the CPI increase of 13.3 percent, or a net loss of 4.6 percent. At the same time, the AAUP/NCES reported the base salary increase for continuing faculty from fiscal 1978 to 1979 was 7.4 percent for all institution categories. This was identical to the increase reported by the Department of Labor for the "white collar manager/administrator" for 1979.* Most other professional groups reported declines in real salaries in comparison with the CPI. While disheartening on a national level, it may be of some comfort to faculty to realize their salary growth patterns have been in keeping with those of many other professionals.

Despite the tradition we have established in looking only at base institutional salaries for nine-month employment, for most faculty members such earnings constitute on average only 80 to 85 percent of total professional income. The additional 15 to 20 percent—the total financial reward associated with the profession's economic status—must be examined, especially when the economic status of academics is to be compared with that of other professionals.

Although the University is their primary employer, most faculty do commit time to a variety of other income producing employment. Some variation in the type and extent of additional income work is found by type of institution but similarities are more apparent than differences.[7,8,11] Discipline differences can be large, but even in the arts and humanities about three-quarters of the faculty earn significant additional income. National survey data were collected by John Minter Associates for *The Chronicle*

---

* While faculty salaries are for the period September 1 through August 31 and other professionals' earnings cited are for calendar year 1979, the difference in the percentages would be slight and would actually increase the salary growth of faculty if measured for the calendar year period.

TABLE 2

AVERAGE SALARIES AND ABOVE BASE EARNINGS FOR FACULTY
EMPLOYED IN FOUR-YEAR COLLEGES AND UNIVERSITIES
1979-80

	Average[1] Salaries	Earnings Above Base w/in Inst.[2]	Percent of Faculty	Earnings Above Base Outside Inst.[3]	Percent of Faculty	All Above Base Earnings	Percent of Faculty
All Disciplines Combined[4]							
Professor	29350	4412	68.2	4212	56.0	6410	83.7
Associate	22726	3440	66.5	2825	51.7	4599	81.5
Assistant	18500	2917	59.4	2254	48.4	3614	78.5
Instructor	16597	2382	46.3	5015	37.4	4286	69.5
All Ranks	23844	3655	64.6	3276	51.9	5011	81.0
Fine & Applied Arts (All Ranks)	21873	2208	46.7	2905	67.4	3520	79.6
Humanities (All Ranks)	22953	2493	59.3	1442	41.4	2940	74.2
Social Sciences (All Ranks)	24553	4200	69.9	2741	57.8	5288	85.5
Business & Economics (All Ranks)	25383	4579	72.5	6827	71.5	9246	88.7
Science & Mathematics (All Ranks)	24662	3953	68.3	2571	38.5	4629	79.7
Engineering (All Ranks)	26861	5154	71.6	5901	65.9	8387	90.4

1 Average salaries are for 1979-80 but were obtained only from those faculty employed in fall 1980.

2 Defined to include extension, overloads, administrative supplements, contract research, summer teaching or other summer payments, etc.

3 Excludes royalties, rents, and unearned income.

4 Includes faculty from physical education, vocational education, home economics, nursing and health, as well as those from areas listed.

Source: John Minter Associates, 1980, *The Chronicle of Higher Education*, Vol. XXI, No. 13, November 17, 1980.

of Higher Education in the fall of 1980 and again in fall 1981. Actual dollar amounts of additional professional earnings (excluding royalties) obtained from the national sample of 2,400 faculty members in fall 1980 (with separation of extra earnings from the primary employing insitiution from those paid by outside employers) are shown in Table 2.[7]

Table 2 shows that there were substantial differences by rank and discipline in above-base earnings during the academic year 1979-80 and summer 1980 paid by (or through) the employing college or university. The more senior the rank, the larger were the supplemental earnings. The opportunities for extra earnings through the institutions are greater in professional, science, and social science fields as compared with humanities and arts, probably in part because funded research is included in this category. Earnings from outside professional work (consulting, paid research, other professional salary or income—but excluding royalties, rents, gifts, investment income) are also greatest in business and engineering. Average total additional earnings varied by a factor of about three—from $2,940 (Humanities) to $9,246 (Business). The proportion of faculty in each discipline earning additional income (internal and external) was generally high, however, and varied by the much smaller range of 74 percent (Humanities) to 90 percent (Engineering). Thus, most faculty do earn supplemental professional income: those in the professions earn substantially more than those in the arts and humanities. The fall 1981 faculty salary survey by John Minter Associates[8] provides additional data as summarized in Table 3. These 1980-81 data conform generally to the same patterns as do the 1979-80 data. Table 3 data were selected by faculty rank and type of institution, since the discipline data for 1980-81 are similar to those for 1979-80 shown in Table 2.

In Table 3, the *All Ranks* summary indicates that about 80 percent of all faculty at all types of institutions earn close to the two-ninths (22 percent) minimally needed to convert nine-month salaries to a full-time annual basis. However, for Ph.D.-granting institutions the *All Ranks* figure (29.4 percent) of total extra earnings is closer to the one-third (33 percent) required to convert nine months to twelve months, assuming three months of additional work. Base salaries (not shown in Table 3) are also considerably higher at the Ph.D.-granting institutions. A higher percentage of faculty at private Ph.D.-granting universities (88.2 percent) earn larger amounts of extra income (37.7 percent of base salaries) than is shown in corresponding categories for public institutions. Noteworthy are the 88.4 percent of all full professors

TABLE 3

ESTIMATED FACULTY EARNINGS BEYOND BASE SALARIES[1]

1980-81

	Professor			Associate Professor			Assistant Professor			All Ranks		
	Percent Reporting Earnings	Average Earnings	Percent of Base Salary	Percent Reporting Earnings	Average Earnings	Percent of Base Salary	Percent Reporting Earnings	Average Earnings	Percent of Base Salary	Percent Reporting Earnings	Average Earnings	Percent of Base Salary
PhD-Granting Institutions												
Public	82.6	$8,186	25.3%	81.4	$6,449	27.1%	75.6	$5,341	27.0%	80.1	$6,744	26.0%
Private	88.4	13,987	40.3	89.7	8,181	32.4	87.9	7,015	33.6	88.2	11,124	37.7
All Institutions	84.8	9,736	29.5	83.1	6,912	29.0	78.9	5,788	28.8	82.4	7,914	29.4
Other Graduate Degree Institutions												
Public	79.4	5,450	19.6	88.2	5,653	22.2	81.7	3,486	18.6	82.6	4,961	21.6
Private	92.9	5,422	19.8	89.1	6,054	29.1	65.8	3,892	21.8	82.3	5,265	24.0
All Institutions	83.3	5,443	19.7	88.5	5,761	26.2	76.1	3,595	19.4	82.5	5,043	22.2
Bachelor's Only Institutions												
All Institutions	76.5	3,289	14.2	88.5	4,022	21.4	78.4	2,928	18.3	80.9	3,344	17.9
Two-Year Institutions												
All Institutions	—	—	—	—	—	—	—	—	—	77.5	4,603	22.6
All Institutions[2]	82.7	4,980	17.8	86.0	4,838	21.7	77.5	3,491	18.5	81.5	4,614	19.8

1 Fall 1981 survey data based on 4,319 individuals, weighted to represent full-time faculty on nine-month contract of all types of colleges and universities (excluding law and medicine, proprietary schools, private two-year institutions and colleges with enrollment under 500). The data here represent combined overbase from within the institution and outside the institution. Outside professional earnings *include* royalties in contrast to the fall 1980 John Minter survey which *excluded* royalties (Table 2).

2 Excludes institutions without academic ranks.

Source: John Minter Associates, 1981. *The Chronicle of Higher Education*, Vol. XXIII, No. 15 and 16, December 9 and 16, 1981.

at private Ph.D.-granting institutions whose extra earnings average $13,987, which is 40.3 percent of average academic year base and amounts to average total earnings for this group of $47,694.

Similar findings come from a study of eight Association of American Universities (AAU) institutions, involving 2,016 faculty on nine-month contracts in fiscal 1978. Seventy-three percent earned an average of 21.5 percent of their base salaries for additional, compensated *university* activities.[12] Here, too, there were large supplemental earnings differences by discipline. Only 35 percent of foreign language faculty received significant overbase, those who did averaged only 12.3 percent above base; comparable figures for other disciplines included chemistry (80 percent, with overbase averaging 22 percent), engineering (82 percent, with overbase averaging 23 percent) and business (87 percent, with overbase averaging 23 percent). Again, rank has its privileges: assistant professors, with lower base salaries, also have less institutional supplemental earnings. Thirty-six percent had no overbase income, compared with 26 percent of associate professors and 28 percent of professors with no above base earnings. It should be emphasized that the data presented in Table 4 provide *institutional* overbase salaries only; adding earnings from outside the institution would widen disciplinary differences.

Table 4 demonstrates the salary inequities among five departments, representative of eleven examined in the study. This table shows that the ratio of summer salaries to academic year overbase ranges from 1.5 to 3.0. The lower ratios of favored business and psychology departments are indicative of higher amounts of overload teaching during the academic year; these two faculties earn more, on the average, yet keep their summers free for other engagements. The imbalance is stark. The academic year overbase in business exceeds the summer earnings of both assistant and associate professors of English and is only slightly lower for professors.

Differences in summer earnings, as indicated in Table 5, are evident for all departments. Generally, average earnings from summer research activities were higher than those received for summer teaching, though high demand in business courses provided substantial summer teaching salary in that field.

These differences in summer earnings may be due to differences in funding bases: government funds have generally subsidized research while summer tuition pays for teaching. Summer teaching salaries are typically paid only for a portion of the summer, while summer research salaries are usually for full-time work throughout the summer. Most faculty engaged in summer re-

TABLE 4

MEAN OVERBASE SALARIES BY DISCIPLINE, RANK, AND SOURCE OF NINE-MONTH FACULTY AT EIGHT RESEARCH UNIVERSITIES WHO EARNED INSTITUTIONAL "OVERBASE" SALARIES (1977-78)

Discipline/ Rank[1]	N	Salary	AVERAGE OVERBASE EARNED Academic[2] Year $	(N)	Summer[2] $	(N)
English	134	20846	1477	(67)	3187	(96)
Professor	54	26311	1958	(29)	4345	(39)
Associate	48	18853	1175	(23)	2852	(34)
Assistant	29	14735	1112	(12)	1695	(21)
Psychology	148	22553	2345	(56)	3506	(88)
Professor	44	29330	3014	(12)	4827	(27)
Associate	54	20368	3249	(20)	2917	(30)
Assistant	48	19135	1303	(23)	2956	(30)
Physics	105	25353	1676	(15)	5116	(101)
Professor	74	28291	2044	(12)	5865	(71)
Associate	21	19116	n/a*	(2)	3255	(21)
Assistant	10	16710	n/a*	(1)	3549	(9)
Business	256	24684	3444	(107)	5154	(145)
Professor	88	29927	4249	(42)	6410	(51)
Associate	92	22985	3225	(37)	4600	(46)
Assistant	58	20446	2523	(23)	4520	(39)
Engineering	438	24528	1685	(154)	5275	(407)
Professor	257	28062	1683	(89)	5806	(241)
Associate	117	20750	1583	(33)	5128	(108)
Assistant	60	17323	1845	(31)	3462	(54)

[1]Instructors omitted.

[2]Mean salaries are for those faculty receiving overbase from source indicated.

*Data omitted: fewer than five faculty in category.

Source: Dillon, K.E.; Linnell, R.H.; and Marsh, H.W.[12]

TABLE 5

MEAN SUMMER EARNINGS BY DISCIPLINE, RANK, AND SOURCE OF NINE-MONTH FACULTY AT EIGHT RESEARCH UNIVERSITIES EMPLOYED IN THE SUMMER (1977-78)

Discipline/ Rank[1]	Salary	AVERAGE SUMMER EARNINGS Teaching[2]		Research[2]		Other[2]	
		$	(N)	$	(N)	$	(N)
English	20846	3126	(84)	1671	(16)	1388	(12)
Professor	20311	4168	(36)	1835	(5)	1462	(7)
Associate	18853	2808	(29)	1618	(7)	n/a*	(4)
Assistant	14735	1598	(17)	n/a*	(4)	n/a*	(1)
Psychology	22553	2441	(55)	4203	(38)	2429	(6)
Professor	29330	4638	(15)	5300	(13)	n/a*	(1)
Associate	20368	2768	(21)	2978	(9)	n/a*	(2)
Assistant	19135	1613	(16)	3576	(15)	n/a*	(3)
Physics	25353	3314	(26)	5586	(74)	2855	(6)
Professor	28291	3943	(18)	6296	(53)	n/a*	(4)
Associate	19116	1919	(7)	3645	(14)	n/a*	(1)
Assistant	16710	n/a*	(1)	4093	(7)	n/a*	(1)
Business	24684	4127	(89)	4505	(76)	932	(24)
Professor	29927	5114	(32)	5061	(31)	1271	(5)
Associate	22985	3694	(34)	3936	(19)	1124	(10)
Assistant	20446	3700	(18)	4296	(25)	289	(8)
Engineering	24528	3756	(191)	4649	(295)	1219	(48)
Professor	28062	3954	(94)	5209	(190)	1400	(27)
Associate	20750	3921	(62)	3989	(74)	978	(16)
Assistant	17323	2930	(35)	2797	(29)	n/a*	(3)

[1] Instructors omitted.

[2] Mean salaries are for those faculty receiving overbase from sources indicated.

*Data omitted; fewer than five faculty in category.

Source: Dillon, K.E.; Linnell, R.H.; and Marsh, H.W.[12]

search earn from 22 to 33 percent of their base salary for funded summer work.

Overall, the eight-institution study shows more faculty in the sciences and professional fields are receiving both academic year overload and summer salaries. Morever, their supplemental earnings typically amount to a larger percentage of their higher-than-average base salaries than do the supplemental earnings of faculty in other disciplines.

The difference between teaching vs. research earnings takes on additional meaning when compared with findings of the Ladd-Lipset survey.[6,11] Analysis of these data showed that faculty who earned more supplemental income did more research, were no less involved in institutional affairs, but they did spend less time teaching and were less interested in teaching than in research. Furthermore, the income variable most negatively correlated with time spent teaching was not supplemental income, but base salary. These results lend weight to an argument that faculty members are more financially rewarded from *all* sources for their research and externally related activities.[13] The conventional explanation for higher salaries of those who are least involved in teaching is that the "best" faculty do research and have their teaching loads reduced correspondingly. Conversely, this argument would imply that those who teach more are poorer researchers, and receive lower salaries because of their lesser "ability." (Although there has been considerable study of the perennial issue of teaching vs. research, the results are not compelling either way.)[14] It may well be that the institutional reward structure has created economic discrepancies which adversely affect the quality of teaching by luring the "best" faculty to more lucrative research and external for-pay activities.

Another aspect of the questions concerning faculty use of time and the institutional financial reward system lies in the total compensation (salary plus fringe) paid by universities to faculty engaged in salaried intra-university supplemental work. A 1980 survey of research and doctoral universities' fringe benefits indicated public institutions are more likely than private institutions to include such benefit payment for "extra" work.[15] Nonetheless, the great majority of private institutions and many publics treat overload and summer as "flat fee" rather than extended contract work (see Table 6). When such benefits as retirement contributions take a "summer holiday," the message seems clear that such work is not an extension of one's regular university activities, but rather that these activities are similar in nature to consulting or other fee-for-service activities.

TABLE 6

FRINGE BENEFITS ON OVERLOAD
AND OVERBASE SALARIES
ALL RESEARCH (DOCTORAL) INSTITUTIONS
(N=182)

| | OVERLOAD | | | | | | OVERBASE | | |
| | AY (9 mo) Academic Year | | | CY (12 mo) Calendar Year | | | AY (9 mo) Summer | | |
	Total	Public	Private	Total	Public	Private	Total	Public	Private
Pay Fringe	58	50	8	52	47	5	83	67	16
Don't Pay	80	43	37	86	46	40	55	26	29
No Response	44	25	19	44	25	19	44	25	19
Total	182	118	64	182	118	64	182	118	64

Source: Linnell and Overall (16)

The recent decline in real base salary income only intensifies the implications of this reward structure. If financial incentives are such that traditional institutional activities appear to be rewarded less than in previous years, while "extra" activities result not only in additional earnings but also in higher institutional salaries, many faculty will reach the conclusion that their universities *want* them to be more involved in professional work. In fact, comparisons of the numbers of four-year college faculty involved in consulting for pay indicate they have already reached this conclusion. According to survey responses from 1962 and 1975, the proportion of faculty doing paid consulting increased from 13 percent to 49 percent.[16,11] Speaking for the AAUP, Hansen has expressed concern at this trend:

> More serious, perhaps, will be efforts of individuals to cope with relatively lower real salaries by seeking other employment opportunities to supplement their incomes. Some of these outside money-making activities may be professionally related whereas others will not be.[17]

He also states, ". . . we can anticipate some erosion of spirit that is bound to affect the quality of performance by faculty members," and warns that faculty may seek ". . . to adjust by reducing the quantity and quality of their work."

Bowen makes a convincing argument that institutional salaries have remained "surprisingly strong" in the face of both higher education's steady state and the economy's rampant inflation. Bowen offers the following explanation of institutions' efforts to maintain higher salary levels than they can perhaps afford:

> There is the belief both on and off the campus, that the improvement in relative compensation during the 1950's and 1960's had resulted overall in the attraction and retention of thousands of capable and well-trained people, that these hard-won gains had been in the broad public interest, and that these gains should not be sacrificed to short-run financial expediency.[18]

Capable and well-trained people rightfully expect wages commensurate with their competence. If institutions are able to increase faculty salaries only at a rate substantially below that of inflation there is a strong likelihood that outside professional opportunities for income will tempt increasing numbers of faculty members to spend more of their energy and time on non-university activities—or even to leave the academy itself.

Traditional efforts to retain talented faculty by allowing or encouraging extensive non-university involvement are clearly counterproductive in coping with a problem that appears to intensify in direct proportion to the inflation rate. While extra-university work may be of significant benefit to both university and society, the basic question involves the integrity and viability of the academy itself and the fundamental allegiance it must expect from faculty. In today's economy, it is increasingly doubtful that the individual who aspires to advance economically as well as professionally could long afford that allegiance.

Qualities imperative to the intellectual community are jeopardized by such a shift of emphasis from membership in the academic community to individual enterprise, yet that shift is positively reinforced by much current institutional practice.

Universities and colleges are now paying substantial numbers of their faculty for work not included in faculty nine-month contracts. Frequently this work is not treated as part of regular university employment in that it does not influence annual review of performance and may not carry the fringe benefits that accompany regular, salaried work. Compensation of some faculty on an annual basis could be possible if the more permanent aspects of supplemental salaried university activities were integrated into the responsibilites of those faculty willing to commit their professional energies to the university on a full-time annual basis. Not all faculty would want to accept the full-time commitment that goes with a 12-month appointment and the institution would want to establish clear criteria for such appointments. It must be acknowledged that conversion of nine- to twelve-month salaries could limit long-range institutional flexibility. However, with a limited number of such appointments and the commitment of these faculty to teaching and/or research, the institution could stabilize and increase revenues and thereby fund better faculty salaries.

Some potentially large new sources of institutional revenues beckon as sources of support for full-time, twelve-month faculty positions. Royalties from patents and copyrighted materials hold great promise, and patents from federally funded research may now be owned by the institution. The communication technology revolution provides a major opportunity for new educational materials. Finally, the possibilities for industry-university relationships, including academic-based faculty consulting, have only begun to be explored. Many schools have private practice medical plans under which the institution provides support services and facilities—and collects all income. Earnings are shared with the medical school, departments, and faculty under various allocation plans. These medical practice plans could yield models applicable to fee-for-service consulting consortia in other schools, such as engineering, business, and law.

Innovation is necessary. Higher education faces distressing problems involving equitable faculty compensation. It is time to explore new forms of faculty appointments that could offer incomes comparable with those offered by non-academic competitors, while reinforcing the academy as the primary focus of the academician's professional activity.

References

1 Bowen, H.R. *Academic Compensation: Are Faculty and Staff in American Higher Education Adequately Paid?* New York: Teachers Insurance and Annuity Association/College Retirement Equities Fund, 1978.

2 Hansen, W.L. "An Era of Continuing Decline: Annual Report on the Economic Status of the Profession, 1978-79," *Academe: Bulletin of the AAUP 65* (September 1979) :2-12.

3 Hansen, W.L. "Regressing into the Eighties." Annual Report on the Economic Status of the Profession, 1979-80, Preprint of the Report in the September, 1980, issue of *Academe: Bulletin of the AAUP.*

4 Higher Education National Affairs (June, 1981).

5 Bowen, op.cit.

6 Marsh, H.W., and Dillon, K.E. "Academic Productivity and Faculty Supplemental Income." *Journal of Higher Education 51* (No. 5, 1980): 546-555

7 Survey data by John Minter Associates, as reported in *The Chronicle of Higher Education* Vol. XXI, No. 13, November 17, 1980.

8 Survey data by John Minter Associates, as reported in *The Chronicle of Higher Education* Vol. XXIII, No. 15 and No. 16, December 9, 1981, and December 16, 1981.

9 Bowen, op. cit.

10 Dillon, K.E., and Marsh, H.W., "Faculty Earnings Compared with Those of Nonacademic Professionals," *Journal of Higher Education 52* (No. 6, 1981): 615-623.

11 Marsh, H.W. "Total Faculty Earnings, Academic Productivity and Demographic Variables." Paper presented at the Fourth Annual Planning Conference, University of Southern California, Office of Institutional Studies, June 1979.

12 Dillon, K.E., Linnell, R.H. and Marsh, H.W. "Faculty Compensation: Total University Earnings at Research Universities." University of Southern California, Office of Institutional Studies, 1979.

13 Dillon, K.E., and Linnell, R.H. "How Well Are Faculty Paid? Implications of the Academic Reward Structure." *Current Issues in Higher Education 3* (1980): 1-11.

42 | 14 Faia, Michael "Teaching and Research: Rapport or Misalliance," *Research in Higher Education,* IV (1976), 235-246.

15 Linnell, R.H., and Overall, J.U. "Fringe Benefits on Overload and Overbase Salaries," *Business Officer* (NACUBO), November 1981: 19-20.

16 Dunham, R.E., Wright, P.S., and Chandler, M.O. *Teaching Faculty in Universities and Four-Year Colleges.* Washington, D.C.: U.S. Office of Education, 1966.

17 Hansen, op.cit.

18 Bowen, op.cit.

4. Professional Activities for Additional Income: Benefits and Problems

Robert H. Linnell

WHILE DISCUSSION OF THE merits and problems of faculty supplemental employment dates to the nineteenth century, faculty obligations for full-time service to the university continue to be vaguely stated in clouds of idealistic rhetoric[1]. According to one view, full-time faculty service requires a commitment and, indeed, a consecration of total energies to the academic institution. Another holds that when academic obligations of teaching, scholarship and service are satisfactorily discharged, remaining time and energies can be applied as one chooses—provided that the institution is not disserved. But what constitutes satisfactory discharging of academic obligations?

A champion of independence, Solomon W. Golomb, professor of electrical engineering and mathematics at the University of Southern California, argues against rules restricting consulting — and, by extension, other entrepreneurial or fee-for-service endeavors. Golomb asserts that in fields where professionally and academically enriching consulting is available, the best people will not come to, or remain at, the university if they are denied both the professional experience and the income associated with consulting. Golomb also points out that consulting is an excellent method of keeping up with advances in the field, is a source of research ideas, and is an efficient means of transferring university research into practice. These are important benefits to which the employment opportunities for students (via the professor's industrial contacts) and the potential for industrial funding of university research and student scholarship should be added.[2]

In a paper discussing industry's views of faculty consulting and research services, Lajoie and Weinberg proposed the following reasons for industrial interest in using faculty expertise:

1) Available, independent, focused expertise;

2) Peer review;

3) Independent communications between competing industry and government; and

4) Credible opinions.[3]

According to Lajoie and Weinberg, faculty time used for consulting or research services is viewed as the property of the faculty member to be used as he/she sees fit. The academician uniquely ". . . is selling the same expertise for second income as is of interest to his primary employer . . . something no industrial or governmental employee may do." Physicians, lawyers and other practicing for-fee professionals constantly sell the same expertise to all clients, but the analogy to tenure-track faculty is not very satisfactory. The faculty commitment for full-time, salaried status lacks definition, whereas for other salaried professionals the work week or year is much more clearly defined. Professional employees in industry and government who are similar to faculty in background and work activity have generally defined work hours (even though they do not punch time clocks) for the usual Monday-through-Friday work week and they also work overtime for no additional compensation. Some of these non-academic professionals do teach college courses for extra compensation, but on their own time (evenings, week-ends, vacations) in contrast with the traditional one work day per week usually permitted for faculty consulting.*

Public opinion polls indicate a general decline of confidence in both professionals and public institutions; faculty and higher education have not been spared. If it is difficult to know precisely how the public perceives faculty and higher education, negative comments have not been lacking in recent years. A feature article

---

*It should be noted that nearly one-third of the research and doctoral institutions responding to a survey on consulting policy do not have any limitations on the time commitment faculty make to consulting. See Kristine E. Dillon and Karen L. Bane, "Consulting and Conflict of Interest," *Educational Record* LXI, No. 4 (Spring, 1980) pp. 52-72.

in the *Chronicle of Higher Education* ran under the headline, "Stanford to be Asked to Return Part of U.S. Research Funds; Professors Spent More Time on Outside Consulting Work than University Rules Allowed, Government Auditors Find."[4] A major California newspaper ran an article on "Moonlighting, Pension Ripoffs by Profs Charged."[5] Another reported, "UC Concludes Professor's Activities Were in Conflict."[6] An earlier review of many of these articles suggested that ". . . following the rapid growth in support for higher education in the 1960's faculty have emerged with a different image in the public eye. They are no longer the underpaid scholars whose commitments to academe are made with some measure of personal sacrifice . . . As in the case of physicians, society has become dubious that the academic professional can act in the best interests of the clientele served when no monitoring of professional activity is influenced by the clientele," that is, students, taxpayers, legislators and the general public.[7]

There appears to be an increasing interest in the outside professional activities of academic personnel. The news media took considerable note of a report that David Saxon, President of the University of California Systemwide Administration, was hired by Ford Motor Company for six days consulting at a fee of $12,000.[8] The news report pointedly stated that the UC president is the state's highest paid official. Many other examples of various degrees of seriousness could be cited. A grand jury has indicted Dr. Stanley Jacob, a professor at the University of Oregon Health Sciences Center and a strong advocate of legalizing the drug DMSO, on charges that he gave $30,000 to Dr. K.C. Pani, who was the official responsible for reviewing DMSO at the U.S. Food and Drug Administration.[9] Fortune magazine, in an article "The Boardroom Battle of Bendix"[10] mentions that one of Agee's (CEO of Bendix) strong supporters was board member Hugh Uyterhoeven, a Professor at the Harvard Business School, who received more than $40,000 in directorial and consulting fees from Bendix in 1980. The article implies that under these circumstances the professor is unable to exercise independent judgment.

A substantial and increasing number of university faculty are financially involved in off-campus for-profit enterprises related to their on-campus research (which is frequently taxpayer—supported). Gene-splicing firms have received the most publicity although many other high-technology areas (especially computer-related) are involved. For example, Dr. Raymond Valentine, University of California (Davis) is a founder and vice president of the private genetic engineering firm, Cal-Gene, Inc. Allied

Chemical Corporation owns a 20 percent interest in Calgene, Inc. Dr. Valentine, a plant geneticist, is using recombinant DNA techniques in attempts to confer nitrogen fixation capabilities to plants normally not having this capacity. He was receiving some research funding from a $2.5 million grant to the University of California, Davis, from Allied Chemical Corporation. Because of the obvious potential for conflict of interest Dr. Valentine was asked to accept one of the alternatives 1) Disassociate completely from Calgene, Inc., 2) Remove himself from support by the Allied Chemical Corporation funding, 3) Resign from the UC(D) Agricultural Experiment Station (where his research is conducted). Dr. Valentine elected option two. Thus he continues both as a tenured faculty member at the University of California, Davis, and as a principal in Calgene, Inc. Although Dr. Valentine continues as a salaried and tenured faculty member, it is the university research that suffers at the expense of his outside business interest.[11]

During the course of the Ethical and Economic Issues project many faculty and academic administrators indicated that serious problems involving faculty consulting and involvement in outside business were rare. Some problems were admitted to exist but it was difficult to obtain information or case histories. This attitude may be changing. A recent news report carried an item "High Tech and the Universities."* The presidents of Harvard, MIT, Stanford, the University of California and Caltech plan a *private* meeting in March (1982) with presidents of a dozen high-tech firms and selected faculty from each of the universities. As stated by Newsweek, participants ". . . will try to agree on principles to govern the complex and lucrative relationships that have sprung up between industry and academe." The agenda includes the following questions: What should be the guidelines for faculty members who set up their own firms off campus? How can the academic community's commitment to pure science be preserved in an era of increasingly commercialized research? Who should receive patents and royalties for technology developed in university laboratories? How much time should faculty members be allowed to devote to industrial consulting? At the conclusion of this conference a statement was issued.**

These are important questions and they need discussion, understanding and answers. But first we need some structure around which to develop these subjects.

---

* Newsweek, February 1, 1982, p. 15, PERISCOPE

** See *The Chronicle of Higher Education* Vol. XXIV, No. 6, April 7, 1982.

Supplemental employment is either internal, by the primary employing institution, or external, by all other employers including self-employment. Although significant and similar ethical issues may be presented in unpaid supplemental activities, this study focuses on paid, supplemental work related to the academic profession of the individual. This second restriction was imposed because professionally related work will generally be more closely related to university work and thus will offer more potential for conflict. Non-professionally related supplemental work could also involve important ethical and economic issues.

The service period of the faculty appointment is pivotal to the definition of "supplemental" income. For simplicity, full-time appointments are considered as one of two types: academic year and calendar year. The majority of faculty have academic year appointments, that is, nine months out of each twelve months, or, on an annual basis, three-quarter time. These appointments involve approximately eight months of actual full-time service, one month of paid vacation and three months of free time available for other, paid or unpaid activity. In an earlier era, the summer months blended into the academic year, and were largely considered time for professional improvement, preparation of educational material and new courses, or for scholarship. This is less common now; the rapid expansion of sponsored summer research funding and of summer school teaching has defined a sharp boundary between "paid" academic year time and the faculty's own "unpaid" summer time.

TYPES OF SUPPLEMENTAL INCOME

Type of Appointment	Supplemental Income Time Period	Employer	
ACADEMIC YEAR	Academic Year	Primary Institution (overload)	
		External (overload)	
	Summer	Primary Institution	Not
		External	Overload
CALENDAR YEAR	Academic Year	Primary Institution (overload)	
	Summer	External (overload)	

Calendar year appointments require eleven months of service and provide one month of paid vacation; these appointments are therefore 100 percent time on an annual basis.

Since academic year appointments require service only during the academic year, supplemental income work is an overload *only* during that nine-month period. In contrast, those with calendar year appointments can engage in supplemental income work only on an overload basis. Issues relating to supplemental income work are identical for calendar year appointees and academic year appointees only *during the academic year*. Summer supplemental income work for academic appointees involves different considerations because it is *not* an overload.

DATA AND ANALYSIS

Data from the 1975 Survey of the Professoriate by Ladd and Lipset indicate 89 percent of all faculty (9 and 12 months combined) report some supplemental income. Only 6 percent of all nine-month faculty and 16 percent of calendar year faculty at doctoral institutions reported no supplemental income. However, at comprehensive universities and liberal arts colleges 10 percent reported no supplemental income (Table 1).

In the doctorate group 55 percent indicated some paid consulting in the last two years, a percentage which dropped to 49 percent when comprehensive university and 4-year college faculty engage in some paid consulting.*

In the 1975 Ladd-Lipset survey, there were significant differences in the first or second largest sources of supplemental income between academic year and calendar year appointments. (Table 1) The detailed data are of interest in understanding how faculty earn their total incomes.

FOR ACADEMIC YEAR FACULTY

Teaching is the most important source of supplemental income, and summer teaching is the most important component of this additional salary. Although more important at comprehensive and liberal arts colleges (summer 55 plus other 14 for a total of 69 percent) than at doctoral institutions (summer 43 plus other 9 for a total of 52 percent), teaching is still the largest source of additional income at doctoral institutions. Consulting ranks second at doctoral institutions (32 percent) and is less at comprehensive/liberal arts colleges (20 percent), ranking the same as all "other" income. At 29 percent research salary at doctoral institutions is just slightly less important than consulting whereas it is only 11 percent at comprehensive/liberal arts colleges. There is a good deal of diversity in supplemental income. Royalties, 18 per-

* See Table 2, Chapter 3, page 31.

cent at doctoral institutions and 9 percent at comprehen-sive/liberal arts institutions, are quite important. Speech and lecture fees are 10 percent at both types of institutions. Only 6 percent of the doctoral faculty and 10 percent of the comprehensive/liberal arts faculty reported no supplemental earnings.

TABLE 1[a]

PERCENTAGE OF FACULTY INDICATING SOURCES OF FIRST OR SECOND LARGEST SOURCE OF SUPPLEMENTAL INCOME[b]

| | Type of Institution and Type of Appointment[c] | | |
| | Doctoral Institutions | | Comprehen. Univ/Liberal Arts[d] |
Source	Academic Yr.	Calendar Yr.	Academic Yr. and Calendar Yr.
Summer Teaching	43%	6%	55%
Teaching Elsewhere[e]	9%	10%	14%
Consulting	32%	44%	20%
Private Practice	5%	9%	7%
Royalties	18%	12%	9%
Speech/Lecture	10%	22%	10%
Research Salary	29%	3%	11%
"Other" Sources	16%	25%	20%
None	6%	16%	10%

a) From the 1975 Survey of Professoriate by Ladd and Lipset, analysis by Marsh annd Dillon, "Total Faculty Earnings, Academic Productivity and Demographic Variables." Presented at the Fourth Annual Academic Planning Conference, Office of Institutional Studies, University of Southern California, L.A., Calif. 90089; June 11-13, 1979.
b) These data all refer to earnings *above* base, academic year or calendar year, as the case may be. It is assumed that a major part of the earnings for academic year appointees is for summer work but the data do not provide this break-out.
c) Classifications of institutions as Research and Doctorate Granting (Doctoral), Comprehensive or Liberal Arts follows the Carnegie classification system.
d) Due to small numbers, data for calendar year faculty were not meaningful.
e) Includes home institution extension.

FOR CALENDAR YEAR FACULTY
(DOCTORAL ONLY)

Most calendar year faculty, assumed to be full-time appointments, also engage in supplemental income work. Only 16 percent of these doctoral faculty report no supplemental income, compared to 6 percent of their academic year colleagues. Summer teaching is not important (6 percent) presumably because institutional policy generally prohibits additional salary for summer teaching to calendar year faculty. Probably for the same reason supplemental salary for research is unimportant (3 percent). However, teaching elsewhere (including extension) is apparently allowable, and at 10 percent it ranks about the same as for academic year faculty (9 percent). In contrast to academic year faculty, consulting ranks first with 44 percent of the calendar year faculty stating it as the first or second largest source of additional income. Speech/lecture fees are also much more important to calendar year faculty (22 percent) than to academic year faculty (10 percent). The diversity of sources of supplemental income is perhaps more important to calendar year faculty. Twenty-five percent report "other" sources as the first or second largest source of supplemental income (compared with 16 percent for academic year faculty).

TEACHING: THE MOST IMPORTANT SOURCE OF SUPPLEMENTAL INCOME

Teaching appears to be the single most important source of supplemental income. Although actual salary paid for summer teaching may be less than that paid for summer research, teaching is the source of supplemental income for more faculty than any other activity; the primary importance of teaching as a source of supplemental income remains.*

The influence of faculty rank and discipline on supplemental teaching income, available from the Ladd-Lipset data,[12] is shown in Table 2.

One-half or more of academic year faculty report teaching as the first or second largest source of their supplemental income. Teaching both in summer and elsewhere is predictably more important at the comprehensive and liberal arts colleges than at the doctoral institutions; there is greater emphasis on teaching at these institutions. Yet even at the more research-oriented

---

* See also Table 5, Chapter 3, page 36.

doctoral institutions, teaching is a major factor. Substantially fewer full professors and instructor/lecturers at doctoral institutions report teaching as of primary importance, whereas assistant professors at comprehensive universities and liberal arts colleges rely more heavily upon it to supplement base salaries. These results undoubtedly reflect economic necessity, availabilty of other sources of supplemental income and intra-institutional rewards.

TABLE 2

PERCENTAGE OF ACADEMIC YEAR FACULTY INDICATING TEACHING AS FIRST OR SECOND LARGEST SOURCE OF SUPPLEMENTAL INCOME[a]

| | Type of Institution and Type of Teaching | | | |
| | DOCTORAL INSTITUTIONS | | COMP. UNIV/LIB. ARTS | |
ACADEMIC RANK	Summer	Elsewhere	Summer	Elsewhere
Instructor/Lecturer	30%	12%	54%	13%
Assistant Professor	51	16	60	19
Associate Professor	52	8	54	14
Full Professor	36	6	50	8
DISCIPLINE				
Social Sciences	43%	6%	53%	13%
Humanities	50	11	52	10
Fine Arts	58	19	61	6
Law	34	6	(b)	(0)
Physical Sciences	42	4	41	12
Biosciences	43	3	49	8
Medicine	(0)	(0)	(0)	(0)
Education	64	15	74	25
Business	44	18	71	20
Engineering	12	5	35	4
Nursing/Health Ed.	42	13	53	18
Agriculture	39	6	(b)	(b)
ALL DISCIPLINES	43%	9%	55%	14%

a) Calendar year faculty are omitted. Summer teaching salary is generally not important to them, although teaching elsewhere, including home institution extension, is more important to calendar year faculty than to academic year faculty (see Table 1, page).

b) Small N, not a meaningful number.

The surprising similarities of the numbers across disciplines, mostly in the 40-60 percent range for summer teaching, outweigh the differences (engineering at only 12 percent, law 34 percent, medicine 0 percent). Even in the "teaching elsewhere" category most values are in the 10-20 percent range. With few exceptions, teaching is the most important source of supplemental income. This conclusion should be compared with the findings that hours spent teaching and interest in teaching were *negatively* correlated with the base salary *and* the amount of supplemental income earned.[12]

Research and Consulting

Faculty at doctoral institutions are more involved in consulting for pay and also in supplemental research work than faculty at comprehensive universities and liberal arts colleges. Academic rank apparently determines opportunity; full professors at doctoral institutions rank highest at both consulting (43 percent) and research (33 percent). In research activities at doctoral institutions, associate professors (29 percent) and assistant professors (25 percent) are not far behind. In consulting, however, associate professors (27 percent) and assistant professors (21 percent) are considerable less involved than full professors.

The increased importance of consulting to calendar-year appointees at doctoral institutions (compared with academic-year appointees) holds true for all academic ranks, except full professor, and for most disciplines. The most likely explanation is that institutional policy permits or encourages consulting regardless of type of appointment (academic or calendar-year year) whereas policy generally limits or forbids calendar year faculty from earning supplemental research or summer teaching salary.

It may also be surprising to note the greater importance of consulting, as compared to research, as a supplemental salary source for faculty at comprehensive universities and liberal arts colleges. Research at liberal arts colleges figures more importantly than at comprehensive universities. At doctoral institutions, consulting is most important in the professional schools, whereas research dominates in the three basic science areas. Engineering is the exception with major participation in both research and consulting.

Other Supplemental Income

All other sources of supplemental income—defined as private practice, royalties, speech or lecture fees and "other sources"—are *in toto* as important as teaching, research or consulting.

TABLE 3
PERCENTAGE OF FACULTY
INDICATING RESEARCH SALARY AND CONSULTING
AS FIRST OR SECOND LARGEST SOURCE
OF SUPPLEMENTAL INCOME

	Type of Institution and Sources of Income				
	DOCTORAL		COMP. UNIV./LIB. ART		
	Research		Consulting		Research Consulting
ACADEMIC RANK	Acad. Yr.	Cal. Yr.	Acad. Yr.	Cal. Yr.	Acad. & Cal. Yr.
Instructor/Lecturer	8%	0%	0%	7%	17%	1%	6%
Assistant Professor	25	5	5	21	29	10	17
Associate Professor	29	1	1	27	40	14	20
Full Professor	33	3	3	43	36	12	28
DISCIPLINE							
Social Sciences	38%	11%	11%	36%	50%	15%	28%
Humanities	13	0	0	10	12	7	8
Fine Arts	7	4	4	15	12	2	6
Law	25	0	0	54	42	0	75
Physical Sciences	46	7	7	26	44	23	18
Biosciences	49	5	5	22	31	37	20
Medicine	0	3	3	0	35	--	--
Education	9	0	0	48	52	6	29
Business	17	0	0	71	50	5	27
Engineering	57	5	5	68	78	16	55
Nursing/Health Ed.	9	0	0	14	42	1	12
Agriculture	28	0	0	65	53	0	20
ALL DISCIPLINES	29%	3%	3%	32%	44%	11%[a]	20%[b]

a)   Comprehensive Universities 8%, Liberal Arts Colleges 20%.
b)   Comprehensive Universities 21%, Liberal Arts Colleges 16%.

Private practice is most important to the instructor/lecturer ranks. Royalties increase with rank—probably because textbooks are written by the more experienced faculty. Lecture fees also increase with rank in importance as an earnings source, presumably because more invitations come to the senior, generally better known people. The "all other" percentages may seem large, and they raise questions as to what the activities are, and how they might influence teaching, scholarship, academic freedom and public service. These questions must await further research.

TABLE 4

PERCENTAGE OF FACULTY
INDICATING PRIVATE PRACTICE AND ROYALTIES
AS FIRST OR SECOND LARGEST SOURCE
OF SUPPLEMENTAL INCOME

	Type of Institution and Source of Income					
	DOCTORAL				COMP. UNIV./LIB. ARTS	
	Priv. Pract.		Royalties		Priv. Pract.	Royalties
Academic Rank	Acad.	Cal.	Acad.	Cal.		
Instructor/Lecturer	13%	11%	9%	3%	17%	1%
Assistant Professor	6	11	5	2	7	4
Associate Professor	5	9	13	6	4	8
Full Professor	4	9	28	18	7	18
DISCIPLINE						
Social Sciences	4	8	24	17	8	11
Humanities	5	4	20	27	2	14
Fine Arts	23	11	16	15	13	7
Law	18	(a)	31	(a)	(a)	(a)
Physical Sciences	1	0	16	29	2	11
Biosciences	0	1	17	15	2	9
Medicine	(a)	34	(a)	5	--	--
Education	0	3	19	11	0	6
Business	7	(a)	11	(a)	18	5
Engineering	5	8	13	4	3	3
Nursing/Health Ed.	4	11	10	5	16	5
Agriculture	0	2	0	10	(a)	(a)
ALL DISCIPLINES	5	9	18	12	7[b]	9[c]

a)   Small N, not meaningful.
b)   Comprehensive Universities 8%, Liberal Arts Colleges 13%.
c)   Comprehensive Universities 8%, Liberal Arts Colleges 4%.

Detailed data on important sources of supplemental income (Tables 2, 3, 4, 5) indicate that although somewhat fewer calendar year than academic year faculty are involved in supplemental income work, the important difference is the *source* of the supplemental income. For nine-month faculty, summer teaching is the most important source of supplemental income, whereas for calendar year faculty consulting is most important; only the "teaching elsewhere" category is comparable for the academic year and calendar year groups (Table 1). Likewise the contribution of research to supplemental income is important to academic year faculty but not calendar year faculty (Table 3). Private practice (Table 4), speech/lecture fees and all other sources (Table 5) are usually more important sources of supplemental income for calendar year faculty, while royalties (Table 4) are less important.

TABLE 5

PERCENT OF FACULTY INDICATING
SPEECH/LECTURE AND "OTHER" SOURCES
AS FIRST OR SECOND LARGEST SOURCE
OF SUPPLEMENTAL INCOME

Type of Institution and Source of Income

	DOCTORAL				COM. UNIV/LIB. ARTS	
	Speech/Lec.		All Other		Speech/Lec.	Other
Academic Rank	Aca.Yr.	Cal.Yr.	Aca.Yr.	Cal.Yr.		
Instructor/Lecturer	3%	8%	39%	35%	4%	31%
Assistant Professor	7	17	16	18	7	21
Associate Professor	11	22	15	22	13	19
Full Professor	12	25	14	28	14	16
DISCIPLINE						
Social Sciences	11	25	10	22	13	11
Humanities	12	15	19	18	17	21
Fine Arts	18	26	29	35	10	41
Law	6	(a)	3	(a)	(a)	(a)
Physical Sciences	9	12	17	21	5	18
Biosciences	10	22	8	35	7	15
Medicine	0	34	0	22	--	--
Education	12	24	14	15	9	19
Business	13	(a)	6	(a)	10	17
Engineering	2	9	14	16	5	22
Nursing/Health Ed.	11	32	26	18	5	22
Agriculture	0	15	35	41	(a)	(a)
ALL DISCIPLINES	10	22	16	25	10[b]	20[c]

a) Small N, not meaningful.
b) Comprehensive Universities 8%, Liberal Arts Colleges 15%.
c) Comprehensive Universities 19%, Liberal Arts Colleges 24%.

No Supplemental Income

By rank the instructor/lecturer group is the largest reporting no supplemental income; about one-third of those employed on a calendar-year basis and one-fifth of these on academic year basis at doctoral institutions depended solely on that salary. Probably many of those in this rank are doctoral students who are occupied with completion of a doctoral thesis. None of the discipline percentages seems exceptionally large.

TABLE 6

PERCENT OF FACULTY INDICATING
NO SOURCE OF SUPPLEMENTAL INCOME

Type of Institution

Academic Rank	DOCTORAL		COMP. UNIV./LIB. ARTS
	Acad.Yr.	Cal.Yr.	
Instructor/Lecturer	18%	32%	12%
Assistant Professor	9	32	10
Associate Professor	7	19	10
Full Professor	3	9	9
DISCIPLINE			
Social Sciences	4	77	9
Humanities	13	19	16
Fine Arts	1	15	10
Law	0	(a)	(a)
Physical Sciences	6	21	17
Biosciences	7	22	10
Medicine	(a)	10	(a)
Education	2	10	3
Business	2	(a)	0
Engineering	0	11	3
Nursing/Health Ed.	11	23	11
Agriculture	6	17	(a)
ALL DISCIPLINES	6	16	10[b]

a)   Small N, not meaningful.

b)   Comprehensive Universities 9%, Liberal Arts Colleges 13%.

At doctoral institutions, few academic year faculty in engineering, fine arts, medicine, business, education, and social sciences have no involvement in supplemental income activities. The largest groups of faculty without supplemental income are the academic year faculty in humanities (13 percent) and those in nursing/health education (11 percent). These non-participation rates are surprisingly low but we do not know to what extent this non-participation is due to lack of opportunity as compared with lack of interest.

THE EFFECT OF UNIVERSITY POLICY

There is strong evidence of the widespread approval by faculty, administration and trustees for supplemental income and the diversity of its sources. Monitoring of such activities ranges from benign neglect or tacit approval to close surveillance in a handful of institutions.

Of 98 major research universities whose policy statements about consulting and conflict of interest have been analyzed: [13]

- Two-thirds have time limitation policies for external activities and three-quarters of them require some type of formal, written statement for approval of outside work. Only one-third require an annual written disclosure report;

- Two-thirds have policies stating that outside activities should not interfere with other academic duties;

- One-half of these institutions have policies regarding constrained use of materials or facilities belonging to the university or requiring reimbursement for their use;

- One-quarter prohibit teaching at another university;

- One-third prohibit or restrict the use of the university name in external activities;

- One-fifth prohibit or limit the acceptance of gratuities or favors;

- One tenth have a policy about constraints on outside activities during leaves of absence or for summer periods; 14 institutions have policies specifically excluding any restraints during leaves of absence or summer periods;

- One-tenth indicate the disciplinary action to be taken for policy violations; barely one-fifth have statements regarding the responsibility for monitoring and implementing their policies;

The 98 policy statements analyzed were submitted by institutions as a part of a study of 168 research and doctorate-granting schools. Of 109 institutions responding, 105 indicated they had some policy regarding consulting and/or conflict of interest; the 98 provided policies for analysis. Since 105 out of 109 institutions had policies this would indicate most do have a high level of interest in consulting and possible conflict of interest.

Given this indication of university concern, the lack of policy for many obviously related issues—use of the university name, limitation on acceptance of gratuities, use of university materials and facilities—is difficult to understand. At the same time, the lack of means to monitor and implement policy (22 of 98 institutions have an established mechanism) and the fact that only 10 of the institutions have stated disciplinary actions for policy violations, indicates a faltering in university response to the consulting-conflict of interest concern of legislators and the public.

Discussion with faculty and academic administrators on a number of campuses confirms the view that policy is generally vague and enforced only in flagrant cases that attract attention. Public awareness of misdeeds on campus may be the crucial factor. Administrators are loath to provide information on case histories, thus making it difficult to collect data on the frequency of occurrence or to weigh the importance of problems dealing with consulting and conflict of interest. Development and implementation of university policy seems largely reactive, that is only after major problems occurred. In view of the many major changes taking place in our society it is timely and necessary for universities now to take some initiative in developing and implementing new policy.

EXTERNAL SUPPLEMENTAL INCOME

Faculty Earnings data from the John Minter surveys for the Chronicle of Higher Education[13] provide interesting additional information. Relevant 1979-80 data* by rank for all disciplines is as follows:

RANK	Average Earnings		Percent of Faculty	
	From Institution	External	From Institution	External
Professor	$4412	$4212	68.2%	56.0%
Associate	3440	2825	66.5	51.7
Assistant	2917	2254	59.4	48.4
Instructor	2382	5015	46.3	37.4
All Ranks	3655	3276	64.6	51.9

* See Table 2, Chapter 3, page 31.

Professors earn on average about the same supplemental income from their institution and from external sources, although a larger percentage report institutional sources as more important (it should be kept in mind that some faculty earn supplemental income from *both* their own institutions and external sources).

For Associate Professors institutional supplemental income on average is about 20 percent larger than external income and a larger proportion earn institutional supplemental salary. The same is true for Assistant Professors whose average institutional supplemental income is almost 30 percent greater than average external earnings. Instructors generally earn slightly more than twice as much from external sources as from the institution; however a larger proportion of Instructors earn institutional supplemental salary than earn external income.

By discipline we find the following differences:

DISCIPLINE	Average Earnings		Percent of Faculty	
	From Institution	External	From Institution	External
Fine/Applied Arts	$2208	$2905	46.7%	67.4%
Humanities	2493	1442	59.3	41.4
Social Sciences	4200	2741	69.9	57.8
Business/Economics	4579	6827	72.5	71.5
Science/Math	3953	2571	68.3	38.5
Engineering	5154	5901	71.6	65.9

There is a rough correlation that the larger the institutional supplemental earnings the larger the external earnings. Average external earnings are greater than institutional earnings in Business/Economics, Engineering and Fine/Applied Arts. Humanities has the lowest external earnings, and institutional earnings exceed slightly those in Applied/Fine Arts. Except for Humanities and Science/Math, about 60-70 percent of faculty in the other disciplines reported external earnings of significant importance to them. Thus, we conclude that the majority of faculty are involved in external earnings activity and that it is of fiscal importance to them.

Off-Campus Businesses

An increasing number of faculty are becoming involved in off-campus business ventures. These involvements include founding companies, serving as officers and directors, being active investors and consultants and participating in stock options and other major financial arrangements. These ventures are frequently in areas of high technology such as genetic technology and information-computer sciences. Large sums of money may be involved and the area of technology is generally related, although sometimes indirectly, to the campus research work of the individual(s) involved. The campus work is almost always funded by some combination of government sources and university resources, or by the very company or industries which have financial stakes in the external venture. The potential for conflict of interest and subversion of the freedom and openness of campus research is almost endless. So far as we know, no national data collection has been made indicating the extent or types of these business ventures. Nor do we know of any specific policies that have been worked out to deal with the many issues involved. Until recently this topic has been almost a forbidden issue on campus. This is rapidly changing and the need for new policies is now being actively discussed.

At a conference on biotechnology held at York University in Toronto in June 1981, Professor Roderic Park (University of California, Berkeley) stated: "Proprietary research has no place on campuses. Students and faculty members must be able to pursue their research where their interests lead them and publish it for their own career benefit." Professor William Dryer (California Institute of Technology) summarized the problem saying: "I think we have to conclude that biotechnology is a second Garden of Eden. The garden is full of all manner of incredible benefits for mankind, but let's hope we develop the wisdom to avoid the forbidden fruit"[15]. Many have not waited for development of adequate policy. For example, Professor Herbert Boyer (University of California, San Francisco) whose research has had major federal support, was a principal in establishing the gene-splicing company Genetech. His interest has been reported as having a market value of $50-100 million.[16] Professor Walter Gilbert (Harvard University, Nobel Prize 1980) has been given a leave of absence by Harvard to help found Biogen, a gene-splicing recombinant DNA firm with headquarters in Geneva. Dr. Gilbert is chairman of the board of scientists and co-chairman of the board of directors of Biogen. He is quoted as stating, "I think of myself as both a businessman and a scientist."[17]

Universities have not carefully thought out how to deal with these problems. Both Massachusetts Institute of Technology (MIT) and Harvard terminated research contract discussions with Middle East governments because of concern about restriction in selection of personnel; in both cases individual faculty were then encouraged to go ahead with the contracts via private corporations.[18] There appears to be a clear ethical issue involved: if it was wrong for MIT or Harvard to accept the contracts is it not just as wrong for the institutions to beg the issue by encouraging their own faculty to take the contracts? The net result appears to have been that the financial gains went to the individuals, not the institutions, and ethical issues were ignored.

Concern has also been expressed about the growing number of scholars serving on corporate boards of directors, a practice which has been referred to as a "pernicious trend" compromising the objectivity of faculty writing on issues of public policy.[19] In addition to service as a director there may be additional consulting fees and research arrangements. Very little is known about these relationships and how they may influence academe. More disclosure and campus consideration of these issues is needed.

Many universities are seeking to obtain major new industrial support for campus research. Harvard University and MIT have been leaders in this area and both have secured new industrial support with novel policy arrangements. Massachusetts General Hospital (MGH), an independent entity affiliated with Harvard Medical School, has a new $70 million, 10 year Department of Molecular Biology funded by the West German chemical company Hoechst AG.[20] Interviews on these campuses indicate that potential problems have not been adequately addressed.*

One of the most vexing problems is that of faculty independence in external consulting and/or involvement in external business and the potential for loss of open and free inquiry on campus. Apparently some faculty refuse to become involved in campus research supported by industry, thus avoiding conflict of on-campus industrially supported work with their external professional activities. Some may have signed consulting agreements with external companies which are in conflict with their obligations to their own institutions or with contractual agreements between the institution and research sponsors.[21] And now, with the burgeoning development of large industrial support of campus research, institutions may compromise the very principles that have given them their unique place in society . Thus there is the dual danger from both individuals and their institutions, that they may compromise the integrity of the university. There is an urgent need for open discussion of these issues and subsequent development of policy and monitoring processes to protect the integrity of the academy.

---

* Interviews at Harvard University and MIT by Robert H. Linnell, Office of Institutional Studies, University of Southern California, Los Angeles, CA 90089.

All supplemental income activities have in common the potential for both benefits and problems. The potential benefits include improved teaching and scholarship through professional growth and public service to society as well as opportunities for research support, student employment and supplemental income enabling the university to recruit and retain good people based on lower (than comparable full-time) academic year salaries (i.e., part-time salaries). On the negative side lies the always present potential for conflict of interest concerning time commitment and intellectual limitations from extra earnings that may direct one's ideas or attitudes, and contribute to secrecy.

Time commitment is important. The choice—working on some activity that provides additional income versus working on basic academic priorities—is a difficult one. Under the double pressures of inflation and disappointment in a basic salary falling behind the CPI, the choice may frequently favor that activity which provides additional income rather than that of meeting basic academic needs or priorities.

For faculty this choice is probably more difficult than for any other profession because it is a personal choice with only very diffuse institutional guidelines and discipline. No other group of professionals is paid what is stated to be full-time academic year salary (inadequate though it may be), assigned a few hours a week (for eight months) of formal work (scheduled classes) then urged (with diffuse policy guidance) to use the balance of its time to improve its teaching and scholarship for the betterment of society. The combination of inadequate (non-competitive) salary and unstructured time commitment virtually ensures widespread supplemental income activity and some abuse. Our data showing this to be the case should therefore not be surprising.

Intellectual conflicts may be less obvious but they are at the heart of the academic enterprise. Cognitive dissonance — the subtle shifting of one's ideas toward those positions favoring personal interests—can occur in the best of minds. Much supplemental income by its nature may be substantially "disposable" income since base salary is usually used to pay fixed or basic expenses (e.g., mortgage, car payments, utilities, clothing, food, etc.) and supplemental income can be treated as "extra." However some supplemental income has become "permanent" in nature, is no longer an "extra," and may exert greater leverage on attitudes antithetical to the concept of the Academy. For example, established government funded projects which have continued for many years in university-managed laboratories and which provide summer salary of up to one-third of basic academic year salary may involve a major commitment by a specific department, such as the physics department at the University of California, Berkeley and Lawrence Berkeley Laboratory managed by the University of California for the United States Government. Such long-term arrangements provide for continuity of research efforts which is generally desirable, but they can also restrict research interests and limit academic free inquiry, especially when the funding has a specific orientation, as it does in this example.

Summer research salary and professional recognition are closely tied to securing external research funding; these facts of academic life inevitably skew research interests toward those areas of scholarship for which funding is available. The more unusual ideas, where there is high risk of failure, may tend to go unexplored.

The credibility of university expertise is another important problem. The societal need for unbiased expertise seemingly has increased as the complexities of modern life become greater. The university has the potential to meet much of this societal need, but the burgeoning supplemental income activities of university experts have on occasion tarnished their credibility. There appears to be a generally increased distrust of experts, and the university is not helping to solve this problem.[22]

Traditional academic behavior, once thought so benign, threatens a major loss to society. A highly publicized example of this took place when the National Academy of Science issued its report *Toward Healthful Diets* on May 28, 1980, stating that there is no need for the average person to cut down on the amount of cholesterol in the diet. Critics immediately pointed out that several members of the panel which prepared the report, including the chairman, had financial ties to the food industry.[23] The *New York Times* editorialized that the National Academy of Science "is supposed to be an authoritative, impartial source of scientific advice to both the public and government—a Supreme Court of Science. But its latest report on healthful diets is so one-sided that it makes a dubious guide to national nutrition policy." The *Washington Post* said that the report "not only has increased public confusion over proper diet. It has also soiled the reputation both of the board and the academy for rendering careful scientific advice." The headline in *Science* magazine expressed the problem very well: "Food Board's Fat Report Hits Fire. Academy discovers Cassandra's problem—what good is the truth if it is not spreadable?"[24] Indeed, if academic expertise is not credible, it is not valuable to society.

It is quite apparent that there is public concern over conflict of interest problems. In the Summer of 1980, the National Science Foundation (NSF) issued a directive pointing out that many principal investigators and others working under NSF grants or contracts to universities also participate in consulting and entrepreneurial ventures. NSF concluded that these activities encourage transfer of knowledge, develop links between universities and industry, and help university and industry researchers in the performance of their functions. They were therefore to be encouraged. But the directive went on to warn that abuses can arise if conflicts of interest lead to: a) diversion of research from the purposes for which NSF support was provided; b) diversion of materials, facilities, or efforts for private gain; or c) withholding the results of NSF-sponsored research from general availability.[25]

Since it is reasonable to suppose that some of the most useful and productive "consulting and entrepreneurial ventures" will directly relate to the investigators' areas of greatest interest and expertise, and these in turn are most likely to be just those areas of interest supported by NSF grants or contracts, this NSF "warning" seems simplistic. There appears to be an intrinsic contradiction which we need to face and solve. The very technology transfer and industry-university relationships which we wish to encourage will inevitably involve the conflicts NSF warns against. In fact it would almost seem that the greater the potential for transfer of knowledge (stimulating economic development and productivity increases) fostered by taxpayer research support, the *greater* the possibility of abuse according to this NSF directive. The system places the investigator in an impossible situation—his most effective transfer of knowledge will almost certainly involve an abuse!

SUMMARY

Data and analyses have been presented which indicate that more faculty are involved in teaching (summers, extension and elsewhere) as a source of supplemental income, than in any other supplemental income activity. During the very rapid expansion of higher education enrollments from the late Fifties through the early Seventies, formal teaching loads were decreased to provide more time for scholarship, innovative teaching, student interaction and service. Trend data are not available but we suspect that formal teaching loads, overload teaching (home institution and others) and summer teaching are all now increasing. We assume that a primary motive in engaging in supplemental teaching is to earn additional income. More than one-half of all faculty report teaching as the first or second largest source of supplemental income and 20 to 40 percent reported consulting and research as first or second largest sources of supplemental income. We conclude that the remaining pool who might wish to teach for additional income but did not find the opportunity is probably rather small.

It has been pointed out that the usual academic year appointment is, on an annual basis, a part-time position. The data in Table 1 (page 49) show that 94 percent of the academic year faculty at doctoral institutions and 90 percent of the faculty at comprehensive universities and liberal arts colleges earn some supplemental income. Additional faculty salary-earnings data from several sources, provided in chapter 3, indicate that the typical "above academic year base" earnings are roughly 2/9 of the base salary. Thus most faculty find it possible to increase their academic year base salary by an amount which very closely approximates that necessary to make total salary equal to a full-time position. That combined salary also appears to provide total earnings, on the average, about equal to those of equivalent nonacademic professionals.

CONCLUSIONS

Although this society has long since lost its agrarian base, the "agrarian" academic year faculty appointment continues on. Most faculty faced with the twin realities of what are essentially part-time positions (academic year appointments) and inflation are successfully seeking and engaging in supplemental income work. The dependence of most faculty on multiple sources of income undermines the commitment to academic priorities and can create apparent and real conflict of interest. These problems in turn can damage the image and credibility of the academy and support subtle intellectual biases inimical to the ideals of higher education.

We should distinguish between the nature of the supplemental professional activity and the income earned from it. The decision to participate or not in a given professional activity has the three elements—ethical, professional and economic. We assume that the individual decision, to participate or not in a given professional activity, will be made differently depending on whether there is payment or not. The academic ideal would seem attainable if professional decisions were based only on academic criteria (value to students and teaching, scholarly importance, professional contribution, value to society, and so on) and not related directly to short-range monetary gain to the individual.

Although a few faculty may be satisfied with academic year positions and salary, the great majority are engaged in supplemental work for an unknown combination of economic, academic and professional reasons. Undoubtedly the need to supplement income is especially important because of the part-time nature of the academic year appointment and salary. Could some of these supplemental economic resources be "pooled" in such a way that the institutions could provide more full-time calendar year appointments at competitive full-time salaries? Would providing full-time calendar year appointments help cope with the concerns about conflict of interest, time commitments and exercise of academic freedom?

Perhaps not. At doctoral institutions the percentage of faculty who *do not* earn any supplemental income increases from 6 percent for those on academic appointment to 16 percent for those on calendar year (full-time) appointment. Thus even with calendar year appointments 84 percent of these faculty members are impelled to engage in supplemental income activites.

Lacking that major block of free time available to academic year appointees, the summer, and the two large institutional sources of summer income, teaching and research, calendar year appointees turn to sources outside the institution. The effect of the calendar year appointment therefore appears to be one of encouraging *more* external-for-income activity, exactly the opposite of what might be expected or hoped for.

The explanation lies in institutional policies. Already paid for full-time services on an annual basis, calendar year faculty are generally not allowed to earn additional summer salary from the institution for teaching or research. If calendar year faculty wish to earn supplemental income, institutional policy, which generally permits consulting and other external activities, requires going to these external sources. This is exactly what happens; a surprisingly large number of calendar year faculty—only 10 percent fewer of the calendar year faculty (84 percent) than of academic year faculty (94 percent)—earn some supplemental income.

If a non-competitive inadequate salary is the primary reason for seeking supplemental income, why do so many calendar year faculty engage in supplemental income work? Two studies suggest salary inequities by discipline exist; some groups of 12-months faculty receive only slightly higher salaries than the average salaries of 9-month faculty.[26] It is not surprising if those 12-month faculty whose salaries are very nearly the same as their 9-month colleagues seek outside consulting and other supplemental income work.

If institutions are to use 12-month appointments to provide competitive salaries, such salaries must be 2/9 to 3/9 above those for 9-month appointments. At the same time, new policies more protective of academic freedom and wary of conflict-of-interest will be needed. Stated another way, if the institution makes a calendar year, full-time commitment to the faculty member, then a greater commitment by the faculty member to the institution *is also required.*

Faculty members in professional fields must keep current with their professions if they are to be effective instructors. It can be argued that consulting in one's professional field is an excellent way to keep current. There is considerable merit to this idea. Professional practice plans, such as those operated by many medical schools, provide a model for other professions. This proposal is outlined in Chapter 8.

There is a need for new initiatives by higher education. Some faculty are needed whose total commitment is to their institutions and whose institutions in return make a full time commitment to them. The detailed nature of these new mutual commitments can only be worked out by widespread campus discussions. These discussions should also consider the status of some current "full-time" tenured faculty whose supplemental income activities are so extensive that their institutional commitment is more like that of part-time instructors. The present concern in *academe* about the increasing number of part-time faculty needs to be broadened to include those whose services are part-time even though they hold a full-time appointment. Above all, as the future unfolds, higher education should be reviewing the diversity of academic services offered via supplemental income and seek positive policies for their integration into the mainstream of the academy.

References

1 Longenecker, Herbert E., *University Faculty Compensation Policies and Practices in the United States* (Urbana, Illinois: University of Illinois Press, 1956)

2 Golomb, Solomon W., "Faculty Consulting: Should It Be Curtailed," *National Forum,* Fall 1979, LXIX, No.4, p. 34-37.

3 Lajoie, M. Stephen and Weinberg, Myron S., "Industrial Views of Faculty Research Services," paper presented at the Third Annual Academic Planning Conference, January 25-27, 1978, Office of Institutional Studies, University of Southern California, Los Angeles, California 90089.

4 Magarrell, Jack, "Stanford to Be Asked to Return Part of U.S. Research Funds," *The Chronicle of Higher Education,* Vol. XII, No. 8, April 19, 1976.

5 Long Beach *Independent,* April 1, 1977.

6 Los Angeles *Times,* December 21, 1978.

7 Dillon, Kristine E. "Outside Professional Activities," *National Forum,* Fall 1979, LXIX, No. 4, p. 38-42.

8 Los Angeles *Times,* November 3, 1979.

9 Los Angeles *Times,* December 19, 1981.

10 *Fortune* Magazine, January 11, 1982.

11 "Academy/Industry Gene Research Plot Thickens," *Chemical and Engineering News* Vol. 59., No. 38, September 21, 1981. The Davis *Enterprise,* February 23, 1982. See also a series of letters and memos and private communications from Dean Charles E. Hess, College of Agriculture and Environmental Sciences, University of California, Davis.

12 Marsh, Herbert W. "Total Faculty Earnings, Academic Productivity and Demographic Variables." Fourth Annual Academic Planning Conference, University of Southern California, Office of Institutional Studies, Los Angeles, California 90089. June 11-13, 1979. A shorter version of this paper has been published, Marsh, H.W. and Dillon, K.E. "Academic Productivity and Faculty Supplemental Income," *Journal of Higher Education,* 51, No. 5, 1980: 546-553.

13 Dillon, Kristine E. and Bane, Karen L., "Consulting and Conflict of Interest," *Educational Record*, LXI, No. 4, Spring 1980, pp. 52-72

14 Survey data from the *The Chronicle of Higher Education* by John Minter Associates, P.O. Box 107, Boulder, Colorado 80306. *The Chronicle of Higher Education*, Vol. XXI, No. 13, November 17,1980: *ibid.* Vol. XXIII, Nos. 15 and 16, December 9 and 16, 1981.

15 Cocking, Clive, "Biotechnology: Too Risky for Universities?" *The Chronicle of Higher Education*, Vol. XXII, No. 19, June 29, 1981.

16 Wade, Nicholas, "Gene Splicing Company Wows Wall Street," *Science* CCX (October 31, 1980), pp. 506-7.

17 Chedd, Graham, "Genetic Gibberish in the Code of Life," *Science* 81, Vol. 2, No. 9, November 1981, p. 51.

18 Henkoff, Ronald, "The Middle East Connection: Do Oil and Education Mix?" *Change* Vol. 9, No. 6 (June 1977) p. 28; Private Communication to Robert H. Linnell from Paul Gray (MIT), May 1, 1978; Private communication to Robert H. Linnell from Daniel Steiner (Harvard), May 8, 1978.

19 Coughlin, Ellen K., "Scholars See Possible Conflict in Academics' Ties," *The Chronicle of Higher Education* Vol. XXIII, No. 8, October 21, 1981.

20 Culliton, Barbara J., "The Hoechst Department at Mass General," *Science* CCXVI (June 11, 1982), p. 1200-1203.

21 Unpublished results. Survey of Industry Use of University Consultants and Part-Time Employees. This study found that many industry consulting agreements require that the consultant assign related intellectual properties (patents, copyrights) to the firm. Robert H. Linnell, Office of Institutional Studies, University of Southern California, Los Angeles, California 90089.

22 "A New Distrust of the Experts," *Time*, May 14, 1979.

23 Roark, Anne "Report on Nutrition Fuels Conflict of Interest Debate," *The Chronicle of Higher Education*, Vol. XX, No. 15, June 9, 1980. See also the *Chronicle of Higher Education*. Vol. XX, No. 18, June 30, 1980.

24 Wade, Nicholas, "Food Board's Fat Hits Fire," *Science*, Vol. CCIX (July 11, 1980), pp. 248-250.

70 | 25 National Science Foundation, "Important Notice to Presidents of Universities and Colleges and Heads of Other National Science Foundation Grantee Organizations," Notice No. 83, June 27, 1980.

26 Private communication, Office of Institutional Studies, University of Southern California. Data from 14 AAU Public Institutions. See also "Characteristics of Doctoral Scientists and Engineers in the United States, 1973," NSF 75-312 A.

5. The Educational Future: Policies for Continuing Education

Kristine E. Dillon

Seeking areas of potential growth for higher education, many academicians have suggested the realm of "continuing education." Interpreted broadly, the term may range from traditional degree programs (generally offered at times and places to meet the needs of working people) to non-degree programs and classes—some from the traditional offerings of higher education, others new to or excluded from that curriculum. Continuing education may also include courses leading to professional updating or certification and degree programs offered for specific types of nontraditional college students at both undergraduate and graduate levels. According to K. Patricia Cross:

> The continued expansion of education to previously un-served segments of population is inevitable. Everyone is going to need more education—women as well as men, minorities as well as majorities, old as well as young, poor as well as rich, handicapped as well as able bodied, hard to teach as well as easy to teach.[1]

Although many institutions are well involved in developing continuing education programs, higher education may not be realistically examining all the issues underlying these expanding educational ventures.

An information-oriented society is creating a growth climate for education in general, yet traditional educational institutions face new forms of competition in this "frontier" of higher education. Even the most traditional elements of the liberal arts curriculum confront strong competition: Television constitutes a powerful tool for teaching the humanities, history, and the arts, and both commercial and public television have developed programs that rival anything offered in some of our finest colleges. This is not to say that higher education's role in this proposed learning society must be diminished; it serves only as warning that the time is ripe for higher education to examine and reassess its strengths and to explore more vigorously the various emerging forms of technological "delivery systems."

Higher education has substantial expertise with which to provide leadership and direction to degree or certificate-related education programs for various professional groups. However, there are competitors. The higher education news media have devoted substantial attention to the phenomenon of American business' development of a "shadow education system," one that currently serves the majority of the country's adult learners. While some cooperative efforts exist between business and academe, the two efforts are largely independent.

Universities may either cooperate or compete with the shadow system. The concern is that higher education as an institution is unaccustomed to true educational collaboration with outside organizations such as business and professional associations. Thus reduplicative programs and wasteful competition will occur. If new forms of cooperation are to emerge, higher education must closely examine the implications of its current policies and practices with respect to continuing education.

Apparent Problems in Current Practice

Institutions face declining enrollments and tuition revenues with inflexibly "fixed" costs for heavily tenured faculties. Optimistic forecasters of higher education's short-term future hope that adult and non-traditional student "markets" may be able to offset declines in traditional student enrollments. But academe cannot overlook the implications of a faculty linked by education and experience to traditional discipline-based and degree-oriented educational programs fitting itself to changing educational delivery systems and differing educational objectives of adult learners. Clearly not all faculty who may be underutilized by existing traditional programs of higher education will find a demand for their expertise in these future programs. Furthermore, given the current operational structure of most programs of continuing education, little evidence is available to suggest that regular, tenure-track faculty are actually taking on assignments in continuing education programs to offset reductions in their "traditional" load assignments. In the majority of such programs, continuing education hires instructors both from outside and inside the academy, paying for specified responsibilities per course taught.

Perhaps most critical within the emerging context of professional continuing education is the fact that many university faculty members are teaching for employers other than their universities—in addition to or *instead of* serving as educators within their own institutions' continuing education programs. Those faculty members in professional disciplines find themselves in increasing demand for their teaching skills and subject knowledge, given the new attention many states and professions are paying to the updating of professional competencies. Health, engineering, chemistry, business, and law are among those disciplines in which university faculty find themselves asked to offer continuing education not only within their university but often through seminars and courses presented by professional associations and businesses. This non-university demand for faculty teaching expertise does not necessarily mean that the faculty member can be accused of entrepreneurial behavior in competition with the home institution. If professional associations, businesses, and other non-educational organizations are seeking university faculty to teach in non-university programs, it is sometimes because the university is unable or unwilling to meet these educational needs itself. Since other organizations are successful in recruiting university faculty to teach outside the institution, it would appear that the absence of a similar university program is not due to a reluctance on the part of faculty to teach in "non-traditional" settings. Apparently the origins of the "consultant-as-teacher" phenomenon lie in: 1) the lack of a university program in the areas for which the faculty member is being recruited; 2) the lack of competitive resources on the part of the university to ensure the participation of its faculty in university-sponsored continuing education offerings; and/or 3) the faculty need to supplement earnings from the university.

Continuing Education and Compensation Policies

The importance of salary policy in continuing education to overall faculty compensation policy may not be obvious. However, as compensation policies and practices are evaluated in light of the recent decline in academic-year (nine-month) real dollar salaries and the multiplicity of sources to supplement academic earnings, continuing education with its lack of traditional compensation policies might well afford compensation for new, regular load assignments.

From one popular perspective, continuing education is viewed as a source of supplemental earnings which diverts faculty energies from regular university commitments.[2] But from another perspective, a commitment to continuing education is but another form of university commitment—and one that may become more prevalent as traditional age enrollments decline and enrollments in university continuing education programs increase. As such, it must be recognized that continuing education has its own share of competition from external organizations which are able and willing to pay faculty and other experts at consultant fee rates to teach their employees, members or fee-paying students. According to Milton Stern, Dean of Extension at the University of California, Berkeley:

> The academic tradition of consulting one day a week effectively weakens the university's disciplinary force and the extension's power to persuade these people to teach (at less money, of course) for university-based continuing education arms.[3]

The involvement of regular faculty in continuing education programs is generally for a specific fee. This fee, modest though it may be, is essentially the *only* reward faculty receive for such service. Little or no academic recognition is given for service in continuing education. This policy must be changed if continuing education is to achieve an important role in academic institutions.

Continuing Education Deans' View of the Future

To examine the potential impact of growth in new educational markets and the impact on traditional faculty, 230 deans and directors of continuing education programs were surveyed by mail for 1) the previous year (1977-1978) and for 2) their ten year projections of the composition of their instructional staff, number and major types of program offerings, total enrollment, and level of centralization of continuing education administration at their respective institutions. Respondents were also asked a series of attitudinal questions about instructional staffing policy issues to which they responded on a five-point scale ("strongly agree" to "strongly disagree"). These administrators form the four-year college and university membership of the National University Continuing Education Association (NUCEA) and as such, represent a large proportion of organized continuing education programs in the country. Of the initial group surveyed, total responses numbered 125 (65 percent).[4]

The purpose of the study was to assess recent (1978) and estimated (1988) enrollments, instructional staff composition, and program emphases in order to determine how realistic an assumption it may be to expect continuing education programs to provide new sources of professional challenge and fiscal viability for traditional faculty, given the current policies of higher education with respect to the instructional staffing of these programs.

Analyses of survey results consisted of a tabulation of median percentages of current and future proportions of program offerings and of the various professional "pools" from which continuing education faculty are drawn. Since enrollment size and scale of program were expected to influence staffing patterns, the respondents were grouped in four enrollment categories: 6000 and under, 6,001 to 13,500, 13,501 to 24,500, and 24,501 and over. Enrollments ranged in size from 150 to 352,336. In addition to a comparison of median responses of the four enrollment groups, correlation coefficients were computed for each of the seven attitudinal questions with the total enrollment and with the total number of course offerings. Correlation coefficients were also computed for enrollment and for course offerings with a variable that measured the level of program centralization on a five-point scale (ranging from all courses offered by the CE office or school to all courses offered by individual departments or schools).

Analysis of the respondents' answers to questions about instructional staffing and program offerings showed that most institutions anticipate only minor changes in the character of their continuing education programs by 1988. They anticipate some increases in their undergraduate and graduate degree offerings and a slight decrease in their non-credit, general interest offerings over the ten-year period. These results were found consistently across the four categories of enrollment size. With demographic projections and trends in requirements for advanced professional certification, these projections appear plausible. They also demonstrate an expectation—at least by public institutions—that funding for non-credit programs will diminish at the statewide level. Results also show that deans expect their headcount enrollments to increase an average of 35 percent over the ten-year period. They project a 20 percent increase in the number of courses offered by continuing education.

While enrollment projections by continuing education deans appear generally optimistic, their projections for increased use of traditional tenure-track faculty do not follow this pattern. From a median proportion of 24 percent of their 1978 programs taught as overload by nine-month faculty, the deans project a barely perceptible increase to 24.5 percent by 1988. These results are not offset significantly by a projected increase of about 4 percent in the use of regular, nine-month faculty for instructional assignments in continuing education as part of their regular loads. Deans also project a decrease in their use of faculty employed full-time at other universities, but they anticipate no change in their reliance on professionals from outside academe as instructors. Instructors drawn from the pool of non-academic professions accounted for a median proportion of 14.8 percent of the respondents' instructional staff in 1978 and were projected to be the same proportion in 1988. While proportions varied slightly across the enrollment groups, there was some measure of consistency in continuing education programs, despite tremendous differences in size and scope of programs.

The correlations of enrollment and number of course offerings with attitudinal responses to questions about instructional staffing policies revealed no associations between size of program and attitudes toward staffing policies. Deans agreed consistently that their faculty should participate in instructional development programs (79 percent) and that traditional faculty should receive institutional recognition in salary and promotion reviews for service in continuing education (92 percent). A majority of the respondents also believed that instructors should be hired on the basis of their expertise alone, regardless of their employment affiliations. Over half also felt their institutions should prohibit traditional faculty from "moonlighting" if this teaching activity was in competition with programs offered through their own school of continuing education.

IMPLICATIONS OF THE CONTINUING EDUCATION PROJECTIONS FOR UNIVERSITY INSTRUCTIONAL STAFF

From the survey results, it appears few deans anticipate substantial differences in their institutions' approaches to the instructional staffing of educational programs for adult students. They expect more students in their programs but do not expect to use very many more of the regular faculty to instruct them.

One reason may be the belief that they cannot compete financially with the consulting fees faculty in professional schools can earn by teaching outside the university. According to John Maxwell, the deans must expect competition for continuing education offerings from the "thousands of individual instructor-practitioners who operate quite independently." Speaking specifically about continuing education in business, he describes these competitors:

These may be moonlighting faculty members; most universities have the experience of individual business faculty acting as independent entrepreneurs in giving seminars, sometimes even to the point of competing with university-sponsored programs in which the faculty member is one of the listed instructors.[5]

Another reason the deans may not expect to make wider use of tenure-track, departmental faculty often is internal competition within the university. Some departments and schools organize their own continuing education and do not coordinate these efforts with university schools of continuing education. Some of the obvious reasons for this "internal" competition are departmental desires for involvement in all education in its field, better visibility among the population served, belief that such programs are more effectively designed and marketed by the department, and opportunities for increased school or departmental revenues.[6] From the standpoint of concern over effective use of university resources and personnel, departmental or school control is not necessarily bad but lack of communication and cooperation among the various university units can result in excessive overhead by duplication of efforts and expenses and lack of coordination in dealing with overlapping student populations and program areas.

Instructional Materials Needed
in Continuing Education

The emergence of nontraditional forms of higher education has necessitated the development of a variety of new instructional materials. In some cases these take the form of written texts or manuals but they also include the development of audio-visual materials, televised courses, and computer software for use in assisting instruction.

The survey of continuing education deans requested respondents to indicate the extent to which they commission such materials and their projections of future demand for them. Since many of these products represent significant instructional tools and often require substantial resources in their creation, the deans were asked if they currently market these materials or expect to do so in the future.

These data indicate that many programs of continuing education are currently involved in the development of instructional materials and even more expect to become involved. There are some intellectual property questions that need to be considered with respect to the professionals (often faculty) who develop the materials.

TABLE 1

INSTRUCTIONAL MATERIALS
COMMISSIONED AND MARKETED BY
CONTINUING EDUCATION:
ACTUAL (1978) AND PROJECTED (1988)

	Commissioned in 1978	Marketed in 1978	Expect to Commission by 1988	Will Market by 1988
Text and Manuals	47%	18%	50%	24%
Audio-Visual Materials	47%	15%	54%	23%
Television Courses	35%	15%	48%	22%
Computer-Asst. Inst. Programs	16%	6%	35%	15%

Tables 1 and 2 show that institutions currently involved in the development of instructional materials follow a variety of policies dealing with intellectual property rights. While many institutions have some type of policy that specifies financial arrangements concerning the instructional materials they have commissioned to be developed, about a third have no policy covering this question. Table 1 indicates that one-third to one-half of the continuing education deans are commissioning or expect to commission production of educational materials; one-half of those commissioning works will also market them outside their institution. Thus a satisfactory intellectual property policy is essential. Table 2 indicates that only 20 to 25 percent of the survey institutions assign all rights and royalties to the continuing education school or the university. University ownership with royalty sharing is policy at 25 to 30 percent of these institutions; royalty sharing only for external use, 15 to 20 percent, is a more popular policy than royalty sharing in all cases, which is 7 to 10 percent. The usual academic tradition (with written policy at many institutions) permits faculty ownership and all royalties on non-commissioned educational materials and works of art, generally with modest or little institutional financial support. However, the survey results indicate that in continuing education only 4 to 6 percent of the responding institutions give the individual all rights and royalties for external distribution and another 1 to 5 percent give the individual all rights and royalties for all uses. We conclude that although there is a serious lack of policy in at least one-third of the institutions surveyed, policy which does exist is distinctly different from the traditional exclusive faculty rights. Commissioned works are more the norm in continuing education, whereas they are unusual in the academic schools and departments. Policy differences in ownership and royalty rights probably relate more to whether the works are commissioned or not, rather than to any difference in continuing education vs. academic schools and departments.

TABLE 2

Distribution of types of intellectual property policies followed by schools of continuing education for: Texts and Manuals, Audio-Visual, Television, and Computer Assisted Instruction.

Texts	A.-V.	T.V.	CAI	
24%	21%	21%	19%	All rights and royalties belong to continuing education or the university.
				CE or the university retains ownership but royalties are shared with originating individual:
20%	21%	19%	15%	1) when the work is externally marketed
7%	9%	10%	10%	2) in all cases
4%	5%	6%	6%	The individual retains all rights and royalties for external distribution.
5%	4%	1%	2%	The individual retains all rights and royalties for all uses.
7%	8%	8%	8%	Other policy than specified above.
33%	32%	35%	40%	No defined policy exists.

Another significant policy issue emerged from discussion of these results in campus interviews and telephone and written communications.[7] Continuing education schools and divisions appear to be hiring an increasing number of non-faculty professionals. These professionals usually have faculty-like characteristics (graduate education, earned doctorates, aspirations to be faculty members) and work assignments are similar to those normally given faculty (organizing and teaching courses and programs, research, producing educational materials, educational administration). Many of these professionals in fact planned on faculty careers which did not materialize due to a weak market. By job category these individuals are considered professional staff: they work scheduled hours (but no time clocks), have defined vacations, and they assign property rights to their employer. They are treated very much like their professional colleagues working in the private sector and in government. And of course they do not have the possibility of tenure. The property rights of these salaried professionals are different from those of faculty. These salaried professionals may be required to assign property rights, including royalties, to their institutions, whereas faculty producing educational materials for continuing education are not only paid to produce the material but they also retain some property rights. The financial incentive to the institution may tilt toward use of salaried professionals rather than faculty. There is the added flexibility provided by no long term tenure commitment. These policies may discourage the use of experienced faculty teachers in the preparation of educational materials.

Conclusions and New Policy Directions

According to Cross, the stakes and risks are high. "How higher education handles the competitive and cooperative aspects of the 'adult market' is probably the determining factor over the next ten to twenty years in who the new clientele for higher education will be."[8] At least in the realm of degree-related and professional programs, the traditional faculty could play a large role in higher education's ability to exert leadership in the continuing education arena. Current practice and lack of coordinated policy in this growing area may well prove seriously detrimental to that role. Stern outlines the situation and its negative potential as follows:

> The university as an institution has no independent policy and no independent set of practical guidelines in continuing professional education. It has consented to be led by professional societies, by faculty members representing the professional who are, in turn, members of interlocking directorates—of licensing boards, and of the high command of professional societies and professional faculties . . . The failure of leadership in this area of policy and ensuing practice will result in the weakening of the complex comprehensive university in our country . . . [9]

Clearly, businesses and professional associations have legitimate concerns regarding the form continuing education takes. But rather than cede all responsibility, higher education has the capacity to cooperate with these external organizations, recognizing them as knowledgeable consumers and collaborators in the design and development of coherent programs.

According to Maxwell, of the more than 30 million continuing education enrollments annually, less than half are in colleges and universities.[10] A news article reports that four out of five of the country's largest companies—those with 500 or more employees—offer employees formal educational opportunities. Although most companies have plans that pay between 75 and 100 percent of the cost of education, only four percent of all eligible workers use the tuition-aid program.*[11] This report estimates that U.S. companies spend about $10 billion a year to provide postsecondary education and training to over 12 million people; it points out that this is comparable to total federal outlays for higher education and involves about the same number of people as total college/university enrollments (and approximately 20 percent of total college/university expenditures). Learning is indeed the most important cradle-to-grave activity, and it involves tremendous resources. Colleges and universities appear to be playing a decreasing role. The electronic-information revolution is still in its infancy and future developments will undoubtedly radically impact teaching and learning. Computers, cable TV and myriad evolving electronic information systems will certainly greatly expand the horizons of human learning. There seems little doubt that this will happen. The question is: Will colleges and universities be defining the frontier or will they continue to be trapped in their traditionalism?

Current college/university practice and lack of comprehensive university policy has stimulated the growth of a disconnected array of courses and programs. Faculty and professional groups with multiple vested interests have feasted at the resulting educational smorgasbord. Bowen suggests that "it is time for institutions of all kinds to fold non-traditional study into their programs—assigning regular faculty and facilities to it."[12] This approach would provide the kind of cohesiveness currently lacking and could afford a better utilization of university facilities and personnel as enrollment in traditional programs diminishes.

Compensation and reward policies for faculty are a critical element to the successful reorientation of practice and policy in continuing education. The role of the faculty member teaching in continuing education is often similar to the faculty member's role as consultant. As such it is not easy to fit activities into the

---

*From Gregory B. Smith, National Institute for Work and Learning, as quoted in reference 11.

traditional evaluation procedures used for promotion and salary review. Nor has it been possible for schools of continuing education to effectively utilize faculty in bold, new, but longer range thinking, utilizing cutting-edge technology and broad program planning. According to Freedman,

> A great deal of continuing education consists of short, dis-
> continuous presentations on the current state of the art, of
> an important piece of new information, of a significant new
> technique. These require relatively short-term involvements
> by several different faculty members ... Faculty committees
> do not know how to assess this kind of contribution, and they
> are accordingly loath to recognize it as a regular teaching
> function.[13]

Similarly, development of educational materials which enhance continuing education's ability to serve new students should be acknowledged as an educational contribution. If traditional faculty members are to be integrated into appropriate teaching, curriculum design, and relevant research and service roles with respect to continuing education, the professional (and economic) reward system must be modified to acknowledge their contributions as academically legitimate and important.

In at least some cases, full-time twelve-month appointments might provide a feasible alternative to the current academic year practice. Where regular faculty are bridging the realms of traditional undergraduate or graduate education and continuing education, their appointments could reflect these commitments and establish appropriate accountability and rewards. Such appointments will rely heavily upon a network of compensation and property rights policies in order for both faculty and their universities to feel annual contracts will benefit both parties. For example, these faculty positions could provide salaries competitive with similar non-academic positions combined with traditional tenure and academic freedom privilege. In return the faculty member would provide full-time annual service, assignment of ownership to the university of all intellectual properties produced (with royalties largely or completely paid to the university) and salary promotion and tenure rewards based on a comprehensive measure of the quality of service (i.e., continuing education service would have the same status and importance as traditional teaching and scholarship). Institutions need to experiment with appointments that incorporate different combinations of these ideas. If tenure and academic freedom provide a uniquely productive and creative environment, this environment should be given the opportunity to demonstrate its effectiveness in continuing education. The enrollment potential for continuing education is promising and the resources generated should be adequate to support expanded academic commitment. But higher education must overcome its self-imposed limitations if it is to play a leadership role.

References

1   Cross, K. Patricia. "Exploring New Frontiers in Higher Education." Presented at the 1981 National Conference on Higher Education of the American Association of Higher Education (AAHE), Washington, D.C., March, 1981.

2   Freedman, Leonard. "The Ethics and Economics of Supplemental Teaching." Paper presented at Ethical and Economic Issues Conference, University of Southern California, June 1979.

3   Stern, Milton R. "Competition in Continuing Education in the 1980s," *AAHE Bulletin*, (December 1979): p. 3.

4   Survey conducted by Kristine E. Dillon, Spring 1979. Office of Institutional Studies, University of Southern California, Los Angeles, CA 90089.

5   Maxwell, John F. "Who Will Provide Continuing Education for Professionals?" *AAHE Bulletin*, (December 1980): 1, 6-8, 16.

6   *Ibid.*

7   Campus interviews conducted by Robert H. Linnell, 1978-81. Office of Institutional Studies, University of Southern California, Los Angeles, CA 90089.

8   Cross, K. Patricia. "Two Scenarios for Higher Education's Future," *AAHE Bulletin*, (September 1980): 1, 14-15.

9   Stern, *op. cit.*, p. 4.

10 Maxwell, *op. cit.*, p. 6.

11 Watkins, Beverly T. " 'Post-Compulsory' Education by U.S. Companies May Be a $10-Billion Business," *The Chronicle of Higher Education*, Vol. XXI, No. 5, September 22,1980.

12 Bowen, Howard R. "Adult Learning, Higher Education and the Economics of Unused Capacity," *Future Directions for a Learning Society*, The College Board, New York, 1980.

13 Freedman, *op. cit.*, p. 7.

6. Intellectual Property: Developing Equitable Policy

Robert H. Linnell

INTRODUCTION

Intellectual properties, those creations of the human mind which may be owned, encompass ideas that are patentable, written and other works that are copyrightable, and artistic creations with market value for whatever reasons. Modern societies have recognized that individuals who create intellectual properties should have ownership rights,* including sharing in the financial rewards of those creations. Society has also generally accepted the idea that individuals may assign or otherwise give away their intellectual property rights in exchange for something of value: a specific fee, a salaried position, or any of a diversity of contractual arrangements involving fees, salaries, royalties, etc.

Questions as to the fairness in the distribution of the rewards from commercially successful development of intellectual property—to the individual, to the developers, to society—have stirred legislation both in state legislatures and in the United States Congress. There is no agreement among legislative proponents; some feel the rewards are unfavorable to the creative people, others that they are too favorable to the individuals. Since taxpayer funding supports a great deal of creative work at the

---

*e.g., the Constitution of the United States of America, Article I, Section 8.

| 84 |

universities, a major concern is for the public to derive reasonable
benefit from those intellectual properties resulting from invest-
ment of public funds. | 85

INTELLECTUAL PROPERTIES AND THE
UNIVERSITY

The academy places a very high value on recruiting and supporting thoughtful and creative people, to whom intellectual property rights are of special significance. Although many universi-
tites have policies that deal with inventions and patents, the
electronic revolution in communications and information management, and new United States copyright and patent laws have
rendered obsolete most university property rights policies developed in the past. There is also lack of adequate policies or
procedures to cope with the complex issues in the copyright of
creative arts, computer products (data bases, software), and educational tools. In some of the latter areas, many institutions have
developed no policies at all.

Difficult questions need be answered in apportioning equity
rights to intellectual property, questions of weighting contributive
factors essential to the creation of the particular intellectual
property. We have categorized these factors as follows:

1. *Personnel Time and Responsibilities.* To what extent, if
any, was the intellectual property created and/or reduced to
practice during time paid for by the institution? This is a particularly difficult question, since faculty members generally have no
defined work hours and full-time effort is rarely, if ever, specified.
Although faculty responsibilities—to be met "on the
clock"—usually include research or scholarly and creative work,
there is no requirement that any of these creative activities
should yield practical, income-producing results. In fact, there is
strong feeling that the intellectual properties most valuable in
the institutional reward system are those that are "pure" or
"basic" and these will be generally (but not always) of little direct
commercial value. Thus it can be argued that the primary faculty
reward for commercially valuable intellectual property is the
personal income it generates since little or no institutional reward may be forthcoming. This analysis suggests that a change in
institutional faculty reward policy might be considered.

This question, both for time and responsibilities, can usually be
answered for non-faculty staff. Staff are paid salaries for regular
hours of work and they have assigned responsibilities. However,

increasing numbers of professional staff (frequently with earned doctorates) are taking on faculty duties, especially in research, though holding non-tenure track positions. It is going to become more difficult to determine if the intellectual properties created by these non-faculty professionals were created using time paid for by the institution or if these properties were related to assigned responsibilities. If students are involved, the question is even more complex. There are two different situations or statuses, which probably have different equity rights: a) students who are paid university employees; and b) students who are tuition-paying participants. Some students may fit in both categories while working on a particular piece of intellectual property.

2. *Facilities.* Colleges and universities provide a very expensive array of facilities essential to teaching and scholarship: computers, software and terminals; libraries and information retrieval systems; laboratories, equipment and lab technicians; offices and secretaries or word processing centers—often high-demand areas—and supporting utilities; and other assistance. One or more of these university facilities will generally be essential in the creation, and/or reduction to practice, of intellectual property by university personnel. (Certainly there will be exceptions: the professor of English who invents a new children's toy in his basement shop or the physics instructor who writes a sailing manual on the weekends.) It will usually be relatively easy to determine which university facilities, if any, were used in the creation of a given intellectual property. What is more difficult to determine is the extent of use and its value. Another question is what facilities, if any, should be provided all university employees at no cost and no obligation.

3. *Materials, supplies and miscellaneous contributions.* Many supplies are almost taken for granted (paper, pencils, pens, stamps, copy machines, etc.) though inflation and inadequate budgets are forcing increased accountability. Long-distance telephone charges, travel expenses and attendance at professional meetings are often paid by the institution in the name of professional development. Other materials provided faculty and staff include consumables such as art supplies, chemicals, and reagents. Most institutions have rather liberal policies and permit limited use of these resources for personal/professional use. Many intellectual properties developed by university employees will be based, to some degree, on the use of one or more of these resources.

4. *Relationship to other work.* The relationship of the intellectual property to university work is very important. Does it

relate: a) to the general field of the creator's academic work? b) to sponsored research or scholarship funded by the university, by public funds, by private foundations, or by industry? c) to outside consultantships? d) to student research projects? e) to teaching assignments?

5. *Development and Marketing.* Does the institution play any role in the development or marketing of an intellectual property created by an employee of the institution, even if only to the use of the university name in a particular marketing situation? This use might also include that of a university office/secretary as a market/development center. The American Council on Education has prepared a memorandum on the new U.S. policy which makes several suggestions including educating administrators and scientists about the new policy and creation of an effective system to "market" commercial licensing of patents.[1]

SIMPLE AND COMPLEX CASES

The five problem areas/questions suggest the complexities of the issues surrounding ownership of intellectual property and in the determination of equities in any income that may be derived from them. There appears to be only one question to which there is almost universal agreement: If the intellectual property is not related to the creator's professional work at the university (and no university paid time, facilities, materials or marketing are involved) then it clearly belongs entirely to its creator.[2]

Equally clear-cut policy issues are presented at the other extreme: the production of intellectual property directly related to assigned university work with major use of university resources. These include the professor who invents a new photoelectric solar energy device while working at the university on a funded project involving basic research on photoelectric processes in the solid state; or the fine arts instructor who produces and markets original ceramic works of art, using student assistants, during regular university working hours, with all materials and facilities provided at university expense.

In the first example the funding agency's policy required assignment of all inventions to it, and the university and project participants accepted these terms as conditions of the funding. In the second case, the ceramics instructor actually pocketed the entire income; when this practice became public knowledge, the university was charged with permitting the use of public funds for private profit. The instructor appeared in the public eye to have behaved unethically, at the expense of the university and the taxpayers.

These examples are unusual in their simplicity. Most intellectual properties created by university employees will involve complex interactions of institutional and personal resources, as well as external interactions in consultantships, professional meetings and the like. Here lie the problems in sorting out and distributing equities.

Traditionally, the academic community has been very supportive and protective of the intellectual property rights of its employees and, in particular, of its faculty. In an earlier era, electronic mass media communications were not available and the current multi-billion dollar sponsored research programs were but dreams in the minds of a few academic scientists. Intellectual commerce was more genteel. Professors wrote textbooks with some modest help from university resources and there seemed no reason to question that full ownership and royalties were vested in the faculty member. To avoid the appearance of conflict of interest, the most discreet faculty textbook authors sold copies of their texts on their home campus at a discount equal to their royalty or, alternatively, royalties derived from their own campus were donated to a scholarship or support fund. (However, many faculty authors have not done this and there have been some campus complaints about authors profiting from their own students.)

Similarly, faculty inventors have produced major financial benefits to their university. Frederick Gardner Cottrell invented electrostatic equipment valuable in control of air pollution while a young chemistry professor at the University of California, Berkeley. When the University of California, the American Chemical Society, and the Smithsonian Institution all declined to develop this invention, Cottrell founded Research Corporation. Research Corporation not only developed Cottrell's electrostatic patents, but has also acquired and marketed patents for many university scientists using the income to make grants for the further support of basic scientific research.[3] Another outstanding example is the invention of the Vitamin D irradiation process by Dr. Harry Steenbock in 1924 at the University of Wisconsin. Since the University of Wisconsin had no administrative mechanism for handling this invention, a group of Wisconsin alumni, with business experience, founded the Wisconsin Alumni Research Foundation (WARF) as an autonomous organization. WARF has been successful in investing its income from the Steenbock invention, and in several other inventions, and currently provides some $5 million annually for support of basic research and research facilities at the University of Wisconsin.

UNIVERSITY POLICIES AND PRACTICES

Many universities have established policies for dealing with at least some intellectual properties. Specific management offices and formal procedures for handling patents have received the most attention, though faculty inventions have not generally yielded substantial income to universities. (The operating costs of some university patent management offices have exceeded the income they generate.)

There are several reasons for this lack of major success. Many faculty have not been very interested in commercial development of their ideas and the university's academic reward system generally does not encourage applied work. Developing a useful patent will usually require a good deal of work beyond the basic research stage. Also government funding is involved in much university research, and the previous lack of a clear, consistent and supportive government policy has muddled "ownership" questions. The uniform federal patent legislation of December 1980 generally gives universities (as well as other non-profit and small business firms) the right to elect to retain title to inventions made with support of federal funding.[4] This legislation has the potential to greatly increase the importance of patents at universities. University patents are not overwhelmingly important now, according to a survey by the Society of University Patent Administrators (SUPA) of 79 research universities and their patents issued from 1969 to 1975.[5] Responses were received from 29 institutions on 498 patents; only 5 percent of these patents had generated income over $100,000 and 30 percent had earned income between $10,000 and $100,000.

A survey of patent policies and patent administration at research universities indicated that in most cases the university patent policy was authorized by trustees or regents, and administered by a research administration office (18 of 48 institutions), a vice-president or dean of research (10 institutions) or a research foundation (8 of 48 institutions). Most had patent committees (34 of 48 institutions) consisting of faculty and administrators (23 institutions) or faculty alone.[6] The patent policies of these institutions generally cover faculty, professional and non-professional staff and students employed by the university. The institution usually takes title to the invention or directs or approves disposition by the inventor. Although 24 of the 48 institutions have agreements with all possible inventors, an additional 14 institutions have agreements with employed inventors, six institutions have agreements with employees only on sponsored research and four have no agreements. Since government policy has required patent assignment by all personnel who participate in or perform work on government supported work, whether employed and paid or not, many universities do not have adequate patent policy. For non-government sponsored research, many universities have no or inadequate policies to cover intellectual property rights.

Most institutions in the SUPA survey do claim equity in an invention based on either the payment of salary or provision of funds and facilities, or both. Sharing of royalty income with university inventors is almost universal, in sharp contrast with the usual industrial employee-inventor agreement in which industrial inventors sign property rights over to their employers as part of their employment agreement, usually with no monetary reward other than salary improvement for superior performance. At the university royalty sharing is sometimes based on gross royalties, sometimes on net income, starting as high as 80 percent to the inventor and scaling down, as the total income increases, to a low of 15 percent. In the SUPA survey the median inventor share was about 35 percent of net royalty.

The inventor's share of royalties seems to be increasing, judging from a comparison of the 1977 SUPA survey with data from a 1962 National Academy study; and the use of a sliding scale, that is decreasing percentage of royalty to the inventor as total income grows, is also increasing. Institutions are also specifying the disposition of their patent income. In the SUPA survey 26 of 48 institutions specified that patent income would go to research support at the institution.

NEW FEDERAL LEGISLATION

On December 12, 1980 the long sought liberalization of federal government patent policy was signed into law. This legislation sets fees, provides for patent reexamination, explicitly extends copyright protection to computer programs and establishes a uniform policy for giving nonprofit organizations and small business firms rights to the inventions they make in the course of research funded by the government. On government projects colleges and universities can now make patent applications and licensing agreements without obtaining government permission case by case. The only requirements are that the nonprofit institution: 1) disclose inventions to the funding agency; 2) file a patent application within a "reasonable" time; and 3) grant the government a royalty-free license. The funding agency may require periodic reporting on utilization efforts and the invention rights may not be reassigned (except for patent management purposes) without special agency approval. Other restrictions are a limitation on granting of exclusive licenses for a time in excess of five years from first sale or eight years from the date of the license (excepting time of delay from regulatory agency approval process). In certain circumstances government can march in and demand licensing (or take ownership) where practical application has not been adequately achieved. Finally, the new law mandates that royalties be shared with inventors (no sharing formula is suggested). Royalty income, after expenses and royalty distribution to inventors, must be used for support of scientific research or education. With the reasonable and simple regulations that have been developed for implementing this legislation (i.e., OMB Circular 124), the potential impact from the large federal funding levels could be considerable.

NEW POLICY NEEDS

The principal roles of the academy—creation of new knowledge and art forms, transmission of knowledge and public service—combine to create a stimulating environment which can also be highly productive in the conception and development of intellectual properties. Societal benefits from application of university creativity include stimulation of the economy, increased productivity, meeting critical national needs for scarce resources, national defense, etc. In addition, university-developed software and data bases are useful in management, economic analysis, forecasting, and myriad other developing applications. University education, training and cultural contributions could also be more widely applied to job training and reduction of unemployment, to creative use of leisure time, to support an improved quality of life and to deal with problems related to standard of living in an overpopulated, increasingly resource depleted planet.

Institutions of higher education generally fall far short of their potential in making these contributions to society. A comprehensive and thoughtful development of an intellectual property policy could enhance university participation in the achievement of these goals.

INSTITUTIONAL AND INDIVIDUAL GOALS

Although teaching and basic scholarship are universally accepted academic goals, public service roles involving problem solving and applications of knowledge have lower priority. Analysis of current policy and practice indicates that classroom teaching and scholarship of a basic nature are almost always institutional responsibilities included in the primary roles of faculty and staff. However as we move toward applications-oriented research, continuing education and a variety of public service roles, these activities all receive less institutional recognition and are more individual professional activities engaged in for personal supplemental financial rewards. Although there are some exceptions and some modest increase in the institutionalization of applied goals is taking place, the commercialization of intellectual property remains primarily an individual professional "overload" activity and is not given significant recognition by the institutions's reward structure.

In view of the new federal patent legislation (and implementing regulations) and rapidly changing technology, universities should review their current intellectual property policies. The increasingly costly university investments in computer technology, libraries, TV centers, laboratories and equipment are creating major financial strains which might be met, at least in part, by income from commercial uses which stem from academic work. Specifically, policies need to treat the following questions:

1. Ethical, Legal and Financial. The policy must meet the ethical criteria of fairness and equity to all participants and it must be in accord with federal and state law.

a) Creator(s) of Intellectual Property. It should be recognized that without creator(s) there would be no intellectual property but the role of colleagues, students, staff, and so on needs to be given proper credit. Determining who are the creator(s) of intellectual property and giving each one fair credit is an important ethical as well as legal problem. Careful, factual determination of individual inventorship participation is essential. Conflict-of-interest situations need to be recognized and dealt with.

b) Institutional Role. Salaried positions and paid-for time to do creative work, supported by computers, libraries, laboratories, etc., is an important if not generally essential contribution.

c) The General Public. All institutions of higher education derive considerable financial support from the general public, directly or indirectly. As non-profit organizations, higher education institutions enjoy many tax advantages, including that of receiving tax-deductible gifts; these indirect public subsidies are of great importance. Local, state, and federal direct appropriations, student aid and grants and contracts provide significant support, in some cases the largest item in the university budget. The public expects a return on this large investment—a return in education, research, and public service. Public interest groups want to be assured that the public obtains its fair share of benefits from this investment; intellectual property rights can be an important area at issue.

d) Legal Issues. The intellectual property rights of faculty and all other employees, including non-paid project assistants, should be explicitly spelled out in an agreement, with the institution, defining ownership and royalty rights. The new patent and trademark amendments act [4,7] now specifically provides copyright protection for computer software (including data bases and computer assisted instruction), thus creating a need for institutional policy in this area. This need also includes the Copyright Act of 1976 since it provides that the employer owns all of the rights comprised in a copyright work (of an employee) *only* if it is a "work made for hire," that is, "a work prepared by an employee within the scope of his or her employment." These legal issues are generally not adequately covered at most higher education institutions, and they should be included in employment agreements and personnel policy handbooks.

e) Development and Marketing. Financial returns can only be achieved if intellectual properties are marketed. Marketing requires investment of risk capital from investors who see a good opportunity for profit. Those who risk their capital require a potential return commensurate with the risk; otherwise they won't invest.

2. Academic Freedom. University policy relating to intellectual property rights should be supportive of academic freedom. Attention should be given to covert as well as to the more overt financial pressures. The individual may be oblivious to these diverse, often times subtle influences.

For example, the selection of a textbook for a large undergraduate course can involve author royalties up to several thousand dollars per year. Although some authors donate textbook royalties from home institution use to their institutions, many don't do this; and institutional policy usually doesn't require this action. The untenured assistant professor, with ideas for reorganizing a course assigned to him (her), currently using a text written by a senior professor (who serves on the tenure committee), is in a very difficult situation.

Another example involves a professor with substantial federal funding for basic research in an area of rapid technology development who serves as paid consultant one day a week to a large firm working in this same area of technology. Under the new federal patent legislation the university may take title to inventions resulting from the federal support yet many industrial consultantships involve binding patent agreements. The professor is in an awkward if not direct conflict situation which might lead him to direct his federal funding along lines supportive of his consulting which could lead to a conflict in patent obligations.

Another situation involves a faculty member in computer science conducting basic research with federal support. As the work progresses it becomes apparent that it has commercial significance in the computer security field, which results in a paid consultantship to apply the work; in the meantime the supporting federal agency recognizes that the research has implications for national security and the National Security Agency becomes involved. Though potentially valuable patents and copyrights could result from this computer work, the mix of academic freedom issues with federal support, consulting, and national security creates an extremely complex situation.

The important point is that faculty members frequently have overlapping property rights commitments—to their institutions, to federal agencies, and to industries for which they consult. The conflicting interests of these three supporting organizations create a problem which makes it difficult or impossible to preserve academic freedom and engage in technology transfer useful to society. The first step in the solution of these problems is for faculty and university administration to admit they exist and to work together openly to find solutions, recognizing the interest of their students and of the general public.

3. Comprehensive and Consistent Policy. There is an increasing variety and value of intellectual properties conceived or created by faculty and other employees of higher education. An institutional policy should deal with all intellectual properties created by all people working for or at the university. It should be comprehensive, consistent, and well publicized to all employees, students, and any others who may be working at the institution.

To implement this proposal institutions of higher education should establish an Office of Intellectual Property Management (OIPM). This office would incorporate existing patent management functions, copyright responsibilities, and centralize the currently decentralized intellectual property management functions currently operated on some campuses by media centers, colleges of continuing education, and others. Because of its potential future impact on the university, the development of an OIPM should be guided by significant recommendations from faculty, staff, students, administration (academic and non-academic), and legal counsel. Under the guidance of an appropriate committee the OIPM should develop and implement policy and procedures for all conceivable types of intellectual properties which might be created at, or by the university with some use of university resources. It would strive to be comprehensive and consistent in its treatment, noting its inconsistencies and areas of omission as purposeful and not due to lack of foresight. The OIPM would also monitor the operation and effectiveness of policy and have the responsibility for suggesting change and improvement. The OIPM would secure patents and copyrights, develop and market them, and administer income according to agreed policy.

A primary goal of the OIPM would be to provide policy to minimize or avoid the potential for conflict of interest arising when the free exchange of ideas might be limited by possible commercial value of intellectual property. A secondary goal would be to bring university research results to the service of society as soon as prudent. A third goal would be to return earnings to the university for investment in additional scholarship which might, in turn, lead to further practical benefits.

This "investment" of income *should not* be based on potential for additional future earnings. William F. Massy, vice president for business and finance at Stanford University, has stated that public and private reimbursement for campus research does not reflect its full value to society, resulting in "windfall profits" to those outside the university, particularly when a new firm goes public.[8] These windfall profits may also accrue to university employees, usually faculty, and the press has reported several cases, particularly in genetic engineering, that involve millions of dollars. The possibility of these large earnings is most tempting to professors and to institutions, but it could undermine the freedom to discuss work openly, a basic academic premise. Donald Kennedy, president of Stanford University has stated the problem very succinctly: "One casualty surely is the accessibility of a large body of significant work to young investigators and graduate students . . .Perhaps even more important, the fragile network of informal communication that characterizes every especially active field is liable to rupture." "To a considerable degree," he told the Stanford faculty, whether the rules remain adequate "to guide us over the more complicated terrain in which we suddenly find ourselves . . . will be decided by the restraint shown by faculty members in the kinds of arrangements they adopt in response to the extraordinary array of overtures they are now receiving."[9]

The proposed OIPM has a continuing and difficult assignment. It seems an unreasonable behavioral expectation for all faculty in a large university to exercise the kind of restraint called for by President Kennedy. The public today is very sceptical of the idea that any professional group can regulate itself, without a self-interest inimical to the public interest. At the other extreme, excessive rules generally prove counter-productive, causing more problems than they solve.

Ownership of Intellectual Properties

Although many institutions currently have employment contracts that specify university ownership of all patents related to university work, these policies have not generally been developed for all institutional employees or others who may work on university research projects without compensation. Furthermore, contracts do not usually refer to other forms of intellectual property developed with university assistance.

Traditionally textbooks and closely related teaching materials have belonged to authors, though it would be unusual that such materials were produced without use of some institutional resources. As new educational and research tools are developed (TV and other audio-visuals, computer-assisted instruction, software, etc.) existing policy becomes more inadequate. There are some exceptions, usually of a "work for hire" type in which faculty members or other institutional employees produce copyrightable educational materials with an agreement that the institution has ownership rights. These exceptions are frequently either ad hoc to a specific situation or restricted to some specialized administrative unit such as an educational media center or college of continuing education. To suggest changing the traditional textbook ownership rights would be quite controversial, but some changes seem desirable, if not essential, for the university to meet the challenges of the new information/education society and the potentials of the high technology electronic media revolution.

Our conclusion is that ownership of all intellectual properties produced with some university resources or related to university work should generally be assigned to the institution. Incomes should be shared appropriately to recognize the contributions of the creators, institutions, sponsors, and the public.

This conclusion is based on several premises, the first of which is the assumption that institutional ownership of intellectual properties will help to separate intellectual and time commitment to production of intellectual property from the goal of making money. Most faculty members have multiple scholarly and educational interests which could absorb much more than 100 percent of their time; the danger is always present that they will opt for those activities with the potential for extra earnings rather than of greatest interest or intellectual challenge.

The second premise is that institutional ownership of all intellectual properties permits an openness which could be monitored by an institutional committee, while personal ownership is private and often secret. Academic freedom and open communication among scholars and students should benefit from the absence of potentially self-serving restrictions caused by private ownership. With institutional ownership, individuals do not have a private financial incentive to maintain secrecy.*

The third premise is management pooling. With institutional ownership of intellectual properties, the institution can more effectively manage the properties, relieving scholars of time-consuming developing and marketing chores for which many scholars may be ill-prepared.

The fourth premise is that institutional ownership of intellectual properties provides a basis for a reward system consistent with institutional goals. At present, rewards for scholarly work (publications, creative art works, etc.) are usually recognized by promotion in rank, reward of tenure, and increases in the basic academic salary. However, the potential commercialization of intellectual property *is usually not* recognized by the institutional reward structure, leaving the primary reward the possibility of personal financial gain. Thus, a basic scientific discovery, reported in the open literature, may yield high academic rewards, whereas the application of the discovery via a patent and development receives little academic recognition. Likewise, a pioneer scholarly book provides professional recognition and academic rewards but the rewards for an innovative textbook are primarily the royalties earned. Therefore, individual priorities may be skewed toward personal financial gain rather than that which is academically important, in effect contributing to a loss of academic freedom. Institutional ownership provides an opportunity for the institution to develop a reward system for intellectual

---

*The Chronicle of Higher Education reported on January 26, 1981 that "a professor of biochemistry at the University of California at San Francisco has set up a genetic-engineering company that is now reported to have a value of several hundred million dollars." The Chronicle article continues, "While the promise of such profits may be alluring to both the individual professor and the university, it threatens to undermine much of what academics have always considered important—the freedom to discuss work openly."

property that is supportive of academic freedom and recognized institutional goals.

The fifth premise is that institutional ownership of intellectual properties would provide income that could be used for institutional support—a critical need in a era of tight budgets. Secretarial services, materials and supplies, computer time, use of equipment, involvement of students and technicians, and other institutional resources are valuable and frequently essential to successful intellectual property development. When the resulting properties are owned by the individuals, institutional resources may be used in violation of institutional policy, an unhealthy and undesirable situation which erodes the academic environment.

Income Sharing

Most major research institutions have established policy for patent income sharing, some based on gross or net income and/or gross or net royalties. Inventors' shares range from 80 percent to 15 percent, sometimes on a sliding scale which decreases the inventor's percentage as total royalties increase.* In the 1977 SUPA survey the average was 35 percent of the net to the inventor(s). Research Corporation pays 15 percent of net royalty to the inventor and 40 percent to the institution, with the balance going to its grants program.[10] As pointed out earlier, the new federal law requires royalty sharing with inventor(s) but does not specify or even indicate guidelines for determining the percentage. The new law also mandates that the institution's royalty share, after expenses, be used for research or education. Currently most institutions split their share of royalty between the inventor's department and/or school and some central university function.

For copyrighted educational materials owned by the institution ("works for hire"), the creators are generally paid salary (on-load or overload) to create the work which can them be used on campus or for other non-income generating purposes with no additional payment to the author(s). If the work is sold or used for other income generating and/or off-campus purposes, many agreements call for royalty payments to the authors. There are many arrangements. In the Flex-Ed program at the University of Southern California, instructors are paid a flat fee to produce

---

* For example, MIT normally shares gross royalties with the inventors, 35 percent for the first $50,000, 25 percent for the next $50,000 and 15 percent thereafter, providing the inventor's share does not exceed net royalties to MIT.

the educational material (which is copyrighted and owned by the university), plus an additional fee for each student who takes the course.[11] In computer-assisted-instruction (CAI), faculty creators of the software are generally paid to produce the program (on-load or overload) and may also receive additional fees related to the number of students who take the courses. In a mass-marketed CAI such as PLATO, the payments to authors can become substantial.

The same factors involved in developing and marketing intellectual property are relevant for income sharing policy: personnel time (paid by institution) and responsibilities, institutional facilities used; materials, supplies and other support provided by the institution; and developing and marketing support. Another important set of issues is also important to income sharing, namely, equitable determination of who the creator(s) of the intellectual property are (faculty, staff, students), and the importance of the institutional and general public support roles.

The special tax-exempt and tax-supported status of academic institutions puts an obligation on them to operate in the public good. It seems reasonable to guess that since employee assignment of job-related intellectual properties to employers is common—with little or no royalty sharing—the general public might expect something similar within academe.

With the new federal legislation which provides patent ownership to academic institutions and requires royalty be shared with inventors, how will the public react to income sharing in a patent of major importance? Suppose a new gene-splicing patent, developed with federal funds, proves very successful and the university faculty inventor shares 35 percent of net royalties which increase to $1.0 million net royalties per year. It seems inevitable that such a case will happen eventually and academic institutions should consider now what the public reaction might be.

During the years of debate prior to enactment of the new Patent and Trademark Law in December 1980, the major opposition was from public interest groups who argued that public funds should not be used to provide private profits. Undoubtedly these same public interest groups will be waiting to see how this new legislation actually works and whether individuals appear to be deriving large profits through the investment of public funds. If this happens, there will probably be public pressure to change the law.

Some faculty investigators have given their intellectual property rights and/or income-share to their institution, as was the case in the Stanford gene-splicing patent. Although this is commendable, the future public image and financial stability of academic institutions needs more protection than that offered by the good will of faculty inventors. However, if the earnings from public funded university research are used to support additional research and education, including funding of faculty salaries or providing full-time salaries by a shift from an academic year to a calendar year basis, a strong case could be presented that this was an investment for the public good.

SUMMARY AND CONCLUSIONS

Stated bluntly, money may corrupt even in academe, and large amounts of money will surely corrupt more than small amounts.

Though any proposal for income sharing may not satisfy everyone, a draft is useful in stimulating discussion and development of policy to meet the needs of specific institutional settings. If all university related intellectual properties are owned by the institution, as recommended, income sharing is recommended as follows:

Income from intellectual properties should be shared with the creator(s) of the intellectual property.

No one income-sharing formula will be adequate to meet the various types of situations which can arise.

In general, the income-sharing formula to the individual(s) should provide a larger percentage when the total income is low and a decreasing percentage as the total income increases.

The institutional share of earnings should usually be much larger than that to the individual(s). Exceptions would be made only when the institution's contributions are clearly small compared to those of the individual(s) and the effect will not undermine academic principles.

The institutional reward system should explicitly recognize intellectual properties (including creative art works) as contributions which merit equal consideration to that of teaching and basic research. This consideration should not be tied to the amount of income earned, if any, but should follow the academic tradition based on quality and scholarly importance.

The institutional share of earnings from intellectual property should be used for education and research purposes.

Effective decoupling of intellectual and academic pursuits, including time commitments, from activities that have the potential for additional earnings, is an important objective. Therefore, the income sharing-policy and the formula that are used should limit the direct extra income to the individuals. The institutional

share, which could be large, should support not only scholarship and education, but should also enhance the economic security of faculty and other employees. As suggested, academic-year appointments could be changed to full-time, 12-month appointments, funded in part by income from intellectual properties. Institutional payments of summer salary would enable faculty with these appointments to achieve salary parity with non-academic colleagues. Institutional income from intellectual property could also be used to provide general support of research and education, including research initiation grants, secretarial support, computers, travel, student stipends, etc. While royalty income to institutions has not been very large in the past, in the future large income is a real potential both because of the new federal policy and the increasing use of educational material and electronic media. However, policy needs to change in the direction giving institution ownership and control of all intellectual properties created by employees and students. Undoubtedly the general public will be much more supportive of the instituion if royalty funds support the institution rather than going to individuals as additional earnings. Royalty from educational sources requires special comment. The newer educational media, largely coming via the electronic revolution (CAI, TV, other audio-visual) are a great challenge and opportunity for higher education. The ideas expressed here apply quite well to all of these new educational media. They should be owned by the institution and income sharing should be substantially to the institution rather than the individual. The institutional income could be used to enhance the economic security of faculty through the institutional reward structure (which must then recognize the importance of educational contributions), including summer salary or by conversion of academic to full-time 12-month positions and to support innovative educational developments.

Institutions must work out what will be sometimes complex details of these new intellectual property arrangements, if the university is to have meaningful academic freedom, open communications and a general environment conducive to new ideas. In the longer time frame income to the institution should add a considerable element of fiscal stability to the institution. These profit-sharing proposals are only to be considered Utopian if one believes that the basic ideals of the academy are Utopian. We believe they are realistic and feasible.

References

1 "Memorandum on Revised U.S. Policy on Title to Patents of Inventions Made by Universities with Federal Funds," Taylor, Chester D., Jr. and Tatel, David S., American Council on Education, Washington, D.C. (March 1982).

2 Some states have specific legislation relating to intellectual property. In California the state labor code specifically forbids employers from requiring employees to assign *non-job related* inventions to the employer. (Section 2780, California Labor Code)

3 Cameron, F., *Cottrell: Samaritan of Science* (Garden City, N.Y. Doubleday, 1952); "Science. Invention and Society. The Story of a Unique American Institution." Research Corporation, 405 Lexington Ave., N.Y., N.Y. 10007 (1972); Harry J. White, "Centenary of Frederick Gardner Cottrell," *Journal of Electrostatics* IV (1977-1978), pp. 1-34.

4 PL 96-517, Patent and Trademark Law Amendments Act, signed into law by President Jimmy Carter on December 12, 1980. See especially chapter 38, Patent Rights In Inventions Made with Federal Assistance. The patent policy provisions of this legislation went into effect July 1, 1981:

5 Woodrow, R.J., Terapane, J., Marcy, W., Van Dyke, N. *Survey of University Patents and Licenses: Preliminary results.* Presented at the Atlanta, Georgia, meeting of the Society of University Patent Administrators, February 6, 1978.

6 *University Patent Policies and Patent Administration.* Princeton University, April 1977, conducted for the Society of University Patent Administrators.

7 Smith, A.A., "Uniform Patent Legislation," *Journal of College and University Law,* VIII, No. 1 (1981).

8 Massy, W.F., "Should We Buy Into Small Venture Firms," *Campus Report (Stanford University)* Vol. XIII, No. 24, March 18, 1981.

9 "Professors Urged to Use Caution in Responding to Commercial Overtures on Genetic Research," *The Chronicle of Higher Education,* Vol. XXI, No. 20, p. 1 (January 26, 1981).

10 Research Corporation, New York City. Private communication.

11 Private communication, School of Business Administration, University of Southern California, Los Angeles, Calif. 90089.

7. Government Research Support: Impact on Ethical and Economic Issues

Robert H. Linnell

IN 1979 THE NATION spent about $54.2 billion on research and development (R & D) of which approximately $5.3 billion (or 9.8 percent) was expended by universities and colleges.[1] Of the university-college share, the federal government provided some $3.8 billion (72 percent). Separating the "R" (basic research) from the "D," the national commitment was $7.3 billion (13.5 percent) to basic research and the balance to development.* The university share of basic research is much higher, $3.8 billion or 52 percent of the national total: the addition of university associated federally funded research and development centers (FFRDC's) increases the university basic research share to $4.9 billion or two-thirds of the national total. Generally, some 70 percent of university basic research is supported by the federal government.

In 1953, the first year of national data collection, the college-university sector reported total basic research expenditures of $110 million, with $73 million (66 percent) from federal sources. In 1979 federal sources provided $2.6 billion in basic research support to academic researchers. This increased funding, about thirty-fold over 25 years, has had a major impact on academic institutions.

---

* These figures are approximate because precise and consistent definitions of "R" and "D" are not available.

TABLE 1

FEDERAL SUPPORT OF UNIVERSITY R AND D[a]

Allocation by Funding Mechanism

Funding Mechanism	Dollars (Billions)	% Total
1. Individual Projects[b]	$1.81	47%
2. Research Centers	.55	14
3. Major Research Programs[c]	.46	12
4. R & D on Agency Problems	.49	13
5. R & D in Large Facilities	.16	4
6. Broad Institutional Support	.26	7
7. All Other	.10	3
Total	$3.83	100%

Allocation by Federal Agency

Agency	Dollars (Billions)	% Total
NIH	$1.77	46%
NSF	.60	16
DOD	.36	9
DOE (Energy)	.29	8
Agriculture	.21	5
HEW (Ex NIH)	.16	4
NASA	.14	4
AID	.07	2
EPA	.05	1
Interior	.04	1
Commerce	.03	0.8
DOT	.02	0.5
All other	.09	2
Total	$3.83	100%

a) Ref. 2.

b) Awards of $150,000 per year or less made to support a small number of individuals.

c) Annual support of more than $150,000, usually to more than one senior investigator and providing support for a broad, coherent area of investigation.

Federal funds expended for university research and development, a total of $3.83 billion in 1979, were disbursed according to the funding mechanisms and by the agencies as shown in Table 1.

These tabulations provide insight into federal funding of academic research. Most striking is the fact that one-half of the support is allocated to individual projects of less than $150,000 per year. The other one-half is almost evenly distributed, one-eighth each to research centers, major research programs (i.e., more than $150,000/year), agency problem-directed research and the combination of large facilities, institutional support and all other. Almost one-half of all the support flows from one source, the National Institute of Health, with the next largest source the National Science Foundation (NSF), chipping in one-sixth of the total. The balance is provided by ten major federal agencies and a number of minor federal sources. This dominant role of NIH funding raises questions of potential undue influence.

INDIVIDUAL PROJECTS

About one-half of all federal academic research support is disbursed through individual projects of $150,000 per year or less. Most of this support is provided to academic institutions for the support of one or a few investigators who have generally made unsolicited proposals for support. Peer review is the usual evaluation process for these proposals and the research is generally of the more basic type in established disciplines, departments or interdisciplinary units.

There are advantages and disadvantages in the current funding system. Unproven assumptions are extensively used both in justifying the current system and in urging changes.

The individual project support system is probably favored by the majority of faculty investigators.[3] Funding from Washington has given investigators some measure of autonomy from local institutional administration. Since academic management has tended to be rather loose, in any event, as compared to industry, investigators have a degree of independence rarely found in salaried professional employment. It is usually assumed that this degree of independence is supportive of the three major goals of research: quality, productivity and creativity. It is possible that the assumption is not correct.

In recent years the federal government has greatly increased administrative requirements related to grant and contract support at academic institutions. The academy has responded slowly and often negatively; Affirmative Action is a good example of gradual accommodation. Until recently the federal impact on investigators working on individual project grants or contracts has not been great. However the recent version of circular "A-21" (Cost Principles for Educational Institutions) from the Office of Management and Budget (OMB) details specific requirements for accountability of federal funds. Faculty supported on federal grants or contracts must report total workload or effort by categories (research, teaching, service, administration) and the percent of effort devoted to each. Many faculty members and institutions objected to these requirements, stating that they would create a vast, costly and meaningless administrative burden. Other faculty suggest that the new A-21 is incorrect in principle since academicians do not conduct research in quantifiable blocks of time, that what the funds buy, according to Professor Serge Lang, is "freedom for the professor and long-range scientific achievement." Unless this principle is accepted, Lang insists, the issue of scientific "accountability" will never be resolved.[4] On the other side, John Lordan, chief of the financial branch of OMB, states that the universities must "establish credibility with the public" since research money comes from "hard earned tax dollars that we have to take away from people."[5]

There the issue rests, OMB insisting upon accountability, academe grudgingly complying lest funds be cut off. But people and institutions are remarkably adaptable, and OMB and universities are coming to an accomodation in which each gives toward the others' point of view.

FEDERAL SUPPORT AND RESEARCH QUALITY, CREATIVITY AND PRODUCTIVITY

QUALITY

If peer review of specific projects assures high quality, peer review also favors individual project support, and probably also "establishment" research which fits easily into an agency administrative category. Innovative and therefore risky research will be difficult to fund and investigators *without* an established background *in the area of their proposed research* will find funding hard to come by.

Richard M. Muller, professor of physics at the University of California, Berkeley, in 1978 was presented the Alan T. Waterman award of the National Science Foundation, one of the nation's top scientific awards. He also received the Texas Instruments Foundation Founders' Prize, another distinguished award.

Dr. Muller's outstanding research was initially declined funding
by the NSF, the Department of Energy (DOE), the Department
of Defense (DOD) and the National Aeronautics and Space Administration (NASA). As Dr. Muller states it, he was able to
proceed with the rejected projects by "circumventing the system."
[6] As experienced university investigators know, there are several
ways to circumvent the system, such as spending funds desig-
nated for one project on another, unfunded project, or writing
proposals on work completed so that results are known and the
new support can be used for advancing new and innovative work.
Of course it is much easier to circumvent the system if one
already has support and much more difficult for younger, or first
time grant seekers. As Muller puts it, "The most fundamental
mistake made by the funding agencies is in assuming that the
ability to write good proposals is equivalent to the ability to
accomplish good research . . . . To require that the solutions to
all problems be obvious before the research is begun discriminates
strongly against innovative work."[6]

CREATIVITY

The peer review system may militate against the most creative
work. Some investigators are unwilling to put their most original
ideas in a proposal for fear that a reviewer may steal the ideas; it
may be difficult even for the most honest reviewer not to be
influenced in subtle ways by ideas from proposal review.

There is also a very real economic problem that has not received much attention. Since most faculty have academic year
salaries (9 months or 75 percent time on an annual basis), there
is a strong economic incentive to obtain a grant or contract that
will provide summer support, usually between 22 and 33 percent
of the base salary. Obtaining summer salary is a high priority
for many faculty in an inflationary era, and as such it will
probably bias research proposals toward good, safe and solid research in fields that fall clearly within a funding agency's support
category. Such proposals are most likely to obtain support and
maintain summer salaries. Clearly this economic pressure can
lead to a loss of creativity. Highly innovative research is also
likely to be high risk research, with a greater probability of
failure; the economic consequences of failure may include loss of
summer salary, in effect a pay cut of 18-25 percent. Since academic-year base salaries have been shown to be higher for research-
oriented faculty (as compared with more teaching-oriented faculty), loss of funded research support may also reduce the academic year base salary.[7]

Younger, untenured faculty (who possibly may have the greatest potential for exceptionally innovative ideas) are under the additional constraint that failure in research can rapidly end academic careers.

Another limitation to creativity is the dominance of health projects in the government support of university research. Although some investigators have shown great "creativity" in trying to relate their research ideas to the health sciences, the concentration of funding in NIH is an inhibiting factor to innovative but non-health related research.

PRODUCTIVITY

The current emphasis on peer review and individual project support is generally believed to be supportive of productivity. More "output" enhances the professional reputation of the individual investigator(s) and improves the probability of support renewal. A negative factor, however, is the administrative burden falling on the investigator(s) when funding is concentrated on individual projects; investigator time spent on administration and government paperwork is not available for research. Productivity could decline also from implementation of new A-21 or related government accountability requirements.

ETHICAL AND ECONOMIC ISSUES

Another set of potential problems involves ethical issues. Many faculty active in research are also involved in external consulting or business activities; indeed, universities are encouraged to transmit basic research ideas to applications useful to society. The "Important Notice to Presidents" issued by the National Science Foundation in the summer of 1980 points out that NSF grantees are involved in consulting and entrepreneurial ventures which can be of benefit through transfer of knowledge and development of university-industry links, and that those relationships should therefore be encouraged.[8] However, the notice also warns that abuses can result if conflict of interest results in diversion of the NSF supported research from the purposes for which NSF support was provided, if materials, facilities or effort are diverted for private gain, or if the results of NSF-supported research are withheld from general availability*.

---

*A review panel of the U.S. Department of Commerce recently stated: "The panel senses that there has been an ever widening gap between

The new federal patent law adds another wrinkle: title to patents from government-supported research is now given to the university to be administered under university patent policy. University patent policy generally provides liberal royalty sharing with the inventor(s) who, under the new law, will have a financial incentive to divert their interest toward practical applications. Individual government-supported researchers will frequently be in an impossible ethical situation; they are encouraged to consult, to transfer knowledge, to be involved in entrepreneurial ventures, to seek practical application and to obtain patents for their institutions. All of these activities may benefit society as well as provide added income to the researcher. It stretches one's credibility, however, to expect researchers to be simultaneously effective in consulting, patenting, etc. (with all the potential for added income) and not divert their government-supported research, at least in some small manner, to serve applied ends and private gain. And it is conceivable that it might be in the public good to do so.

The problem appears to lie as much in the conflicting policies as in individual behavior. On the one extreme, some researchers will refuse to be involved in consulting or entrepreneurial ventures or patents, in order to avoid the potential for conflict of interest; in these cases, obviously no societal benefit through industry-university ties or knowledge transfer will take place. Society is the loser. At the other extreme, some researchers may become so enthusiastically involved in consulting, or external ventures or patent applications that they seriously divert their government-supported research toward goals more supportive of their own personal gain than of the original intent of the grant or contract. Although this latter situation would certainly be considered unethical and subversive of university goals, there appears to be no *a priori* way to determine whether such behavior would result in a gain to society through an important new development or loss because a basic (not immediately practical) discovery was missed. Further, how do we weigh society's loss if the concept of the academy as a pathfinder is subverted in the public mind. Dr. Donald Kennedy, President of Stanford University, in a letter to the Stanford Academic Council, has commented succinctly on

---

the university and industrial communities and as a result this key national source of new technological knowledge is not being adequately tapped for its innovative potential by the private sector—the sector with a major responsibility for innovation in the United States." Advisory Committee on Industrial Innovation, *Domestic Policy Review, Final Report*, (Washington, D.C., U.S. Department of Commerce, 1979).

these problems as related to commercial gene-splicing. Urging caution and restraint in responding to the "extraordinary array of overtures" some faculty are receiving in the commercialization of recombinant DNA, Kennedy stated:

> There is a great need for caution and deliberation in undertaking individual commitment. No one has yet tried, in a serious way, to measure the collective impact of a dramatic increase in outside, proprietary relationships on the part of our best biomedical scientists—let alone of scholars in other disciplines who happen not yet to be in the vanguard. The work that is of value today will be of value tomorrow; it does not need to be locked up by a rush to commercial affiliation. We have time to consider the costs and benefits carefully, to study the adequacy of our own rules, and, above all, to ponder carefully what values we want to conserve in the arrangements we make. I have pledged Stanford to institutional care and caution in this regard, and I call on faculty members to exercise those same qualities in decisions they are being called upon to make as individuals.[9]

Dr. Kennedy then proposed three general principles governing the university's position in commercialization of research discoveries:

> First, and of supreme importance, we want to preserve the values of access and free exchange that characterize a vigorous academic society;

> Second, we are anxious to conduct ourselves in such a way as to bring the fruits of Stanford innovation into human service as rapidly as we responsibly can; and

> Finally, we are disposed to be cautious in getting the institution involved in an equity position with respect to the products of faculty research because of the potential conflicts of interest such a position might generate.

Because of the new legislation giving universities the patent rights resulting from federally supported research, colleges and universities have a major new opportunity to serve the public interest by knowledge transfer, thus stimulating the economy, improving productivity, and encouraging development of new materials, goods and services. At the same time, they may serve university goals, for income from development of taxpayer-supported discoveries could provide a significant increase in funding for university research. But we must not subvert academic freedom. The external threat is that, if a few faculty or other employees of research universities earn large sums personally, as a result of inventions related to federally sponsored research, public interest groups will clamor for changes in the patent ownership legislation.

Many of the current problems associated with federal support could be better handled or eliminated by making longer-term federal research commitments to institutions, with responsibility for management placed *on the university*. Numerous examples of this type of federal funding to industry or specific research centers provide valuable experience for planning more extensive funding of this type. A recent report of the National Commission on Research provides an excellent summary of funding mechanisms and alternatives, in particular recommending experimentation with grants-in-aid managed at the local level.[11] The Commission also recommends that government and universities work together to develop or adopt funding mechanisms that sustain the research capacity to undertake new research initiatives.

Worthy alternatives to the dominant funding pattern exist. A recent study compares research "products" from 20 institutionally funded Materials Research Laboratories (MRL's) with similar products from individually funded materials research projects at 15 universities.[12] Performance was measured by peer review and citation frequency analysis of publication, subjective evaluation of research achievements and research reputation by a panel of experts as well as review of equipment purchases and utilization and analysis of administrative costs. This study concluded that there are no significant differences between MRL's and individually funded materials research projects with respect to innovation, interdisciplinarity, utilization of specialized equipment, concentration of funding, rate of staff turnover, level of effort per research paper and duration of support for research areas. The MRL's appear to be more productive in terms of a greater number of major achievements, however, and they attract researchers with higher reputations. MRL's also involve much less total (federal plus university) administrative cost per grant dollar than do project grants. Finally, in terms of program oversight, the MRL program administration at NSF stresses evaluation of accomplishment, whereas project grants put emphasis on proposal evaluation.

The peer review system, as used by NSF, has recently been questioned. A summary of this research states:

> An experiment in which 150 proposals submitted to the National Science Foundation were evaluated independently by a new set of reviewers indicates that getting a research grant depends to a significant extent on chance. The degree of disagreement within the population of eligible reviewers is such that whether or not a proposal is funded depends in a

large proportion of cases upon which reviewers happen to be selected for it. No evidence of systematic bias in the selection of NSF reviewers was found.[13]

Although this research on the peer review system has been criticized [14] the work does provide significant support for raising some troublesome questions.* To the extent that this research is a valid criticism of peer review of research proposals it would seem also to support institutional funding. One assumption is that peer review of research accomplishments is more effective than that of research ideas (proposals). However, there are alternative mechanisms for funding decisions on institutional support as well as for individual project support.

Dr. A. Carl Leopold has suggested that the paper-work burden of competitive grants from the principal federal granting agencies represented the entire research time of 6,600 academic persons in 1978. This estimate included time for writing and reviewing proposals. He asks: ". . . perhaps it is now appropriate to ask whether Szilard's fanciful story is turning into a serious matter.** Should consideration be given to ways of providing research support without adding to the heavy burden of our present grants and contracts system?"[15]

Together these results are strongly supportive of institutional funding and should encourage federal agencies to expand such funding with a concomitant decrease in individual project funding. Institutional grants could be made to major coherent areas or programs (departments, inter- or trans-discipline groups) and even to major administrative units such as a school. Grants would provide step-funding for a three- to five-year period, with an annual evaluation review based on research progress. Step-fund-

---

*The author of this chapter, Robert H. Linnell, was a program officer at NSF 1962-69. His interest is indicated by preliminary and unpublished work he did at NSF in 1963-64 in which the same proposals were sent to two different sets of qualified reviewers. Results indicated that the reviewer ratings and the subseqent decision, support or decline, depended on the particular reviewers selected. There appeared to be no evidence that the substance of the review or the actual rating correlated with the eminence of the reviewer but it was well known amongst NSF program officers that some reviewers were "tough" and others were "softhearted." However, at that time NSF management decided not to pursue serious research on the peer review system.

**In this story Szilard suggested that if one wanted to bring research progress to a stand still one would invent a competitive grant system requiring individual written proposals with a concomitant review system such that all the researcher's time would be used writing and reviewing proposals. L. Szilard, "The Voice of the Dolphins, and Other Stories" Simon and Schuster, (New York, 1961) p. 100.

ing over several years provides a mechanism to reduce funding for unsatisfactory progress and thereby helps to maintain high quality work and progress. Alternatively, funding could be increased for exceptional accomplishment. A time period of five years is preferred, which under step-funding would initially commit 300 percent. The funding would be apportioned over the five years 100 percent, 80 percent, 60 percent, 40 percent, 20 percent of the first year's support. At the end of the first year, unsatisfactory progress would provide 80 percent of the first year's support for the second year, whereas satisfactory progress (without increased funding) could provide 100 percent of the first year's support to be distributed over the following four years to bring the grant back to its original funding levels. Institutional step-funded grants should cope with several problems:

1. Research results, rather than proposed research will be emphasized.

2. Institutions will be able to provide funding for unusual research that does not fit program categories and to support risky, highly innovative research.

3. Some funding could be provided to institutions on a broader basis than that of a single discipline.

4. Administrative costs, as a fraction of total expenditures, can be reduced. Administrators can relieve productive researchers of administrative burdens.

5. Faculty researchers on academic contracts can plan on summer salary (and thus a full-time twelve-month position) for several years ahead.

6. Research can be planned for several years in advance.

Institutional support will not necessarily solve the problems related to defining full-time effort or of patents and property rights. These are more complex issues, but we suspect that legislators and the public will want some evidence that full-time faculty effort is equivalent to that generally accepted in our society, such as the 40-hour workweek. On this basis, those faculty who work four days per week and consult on the fifth day could be considered 80 percent of full-time and paid accordingly.

The patent-property rights question is more difficult. The extent to which faculty inventor(s) share in patent income may become an issue of public policy. Since the public has paid taxes used to support the research and the faculty inventor(s) were paid salary to conduct the research, it might be argued that all income—as in private industry—should go to the institution to be used for support of additional research. On the other hand, many argue that university policies which share patent income with faculty inventors, in some cases 50 percent or more, provide a desirable incentive. Another difficult issue is that of the faculty member who consults outside the university in a field related to government-funded research at the university. If new ideas evolve that have practical application, which certainly will happen, the faculty member may have a serious conflict-of-interest in balancing equities between the consultant client and the employing university.*

There are no simple answers, but university and government policies are needed which will encourage the application and use of research ideas from the university without undermining the environment of openness and unfettered intellectual discussions so vital to the university's contribution to society. These questions are discussed more broadly in the concluding chapter which follows.

---

*A major rationale for public support of basic research is that providing creative people with unfettered support will advance basic knowledge from which unpredictable practical applications, of benefit to society, will result.

1   "Academic Science, 1972-77. R and D Funds, Scientists and Engineers, Graduate Enrollment and Support," National Science Foundation, Washington, D.C., June 1980, NSF 80-313.

2   "Funding Mechanisms: Balancing Objectives and Resources in University Research," National Commission on Research, 2600 Virginia Ave., N.W., Washington, D.C. 20037, May 1980.

3   *Ibid.*, p. 12. "Individual investigators have mixed feelings about general research support. While they recognize the importance of the needs it addresses, they fear expansion of general research support at the expense of project support. Their primary concerns are quality assurance and *preservation of the relative independence which their relationship with external sponsors provide.*" (Emphasis added)

4   Lange, professor of mathematics at Yale University, is quoted in *The Chronicle of Higher Education*, October 20, 1980, p. 15.

5   "Universities Face New Accounting Rules," *Science* CCX (October 3, 1980), pp. 34-36.

6   Muller, R.A., "Innovation and Scientific Funding," *Science* CCIX (August 22, 1980), pp. 880-883.

7   Marsh, H.W., "Total Faculty Earnings, Academic Productivity and Demographic Variables." Paper presented at the Fourth Annual Academic Planning Conference, University of Southern California, Office of Institutional Studies, Los Angeles, June, 1979.

8   National Science Foundation, "Important Notice to Presidents of Universities and Colleges and Heads of Other National Science Foundation Grantee Organizations," Notice No. 83, June 27, 1980.

9   Kennedy, Donald, "Kennedy Urges Caution on Commercial Gene-Splicing," *The Stanford Campus Report*, Vol. XIII, No. 15 (January 14, 1981) pp. 1 and 24.

10 "Professors Urged to Use Caution in Responding to Commercial Overtures on Genetic Research," *The Chronicle of Higher Education*, January 26, 1981, pp. 1 and 4.

11 "Funding Mechanisms," *op. cit.*, p. 31ff.

12 Ling, James G. and Hand, Mary Ann, "Federal Funding in Materials Research," *Science* CCIX (September 12, 1980), pp. 1203-1207.

116 | 13 Cole, S., Cole, J.R. and Simon, G.A., "Chance and Consenus in Peer Review," *Science* CCXIV (November 20, 1981), pp. 881-886.

14 Letter Section, *Science* CCXV (January 22, 1982), pp. 344-348.

15 Leopold, A.C., "The Burden of Competitive Grants," *Science* CCIII, (February 16, 1979), Guest Editorial.

8. The University's Future: Summary, Recommendations and Conclusions

Robert H. Linnell

IT SEEMS CLEAR that we are living in a world of growing complexities, much of which results from the successes of education and research. Many are bewildered by the pace of change and dislocated by the unanticipated results from application of more new knowledge than any previous society ever dreamed of attaining. The problem is not the new knowledge itself, rather it is learning how to use it for the benefit of humankind. And we need to learn how to educate for change so that we can participate in the excitement of new ideas and yet not be threatened by the rapidity of shifting events. We must recognize that our current education and knowledge bases are considerable assets; higher education should carefully study how it can most wisely build on them to contribute further to the development of an ever-evolving society. However, the halting response of colleges and universities to their current challenges leaves the future in doubt.

The credibility and integrity of the academic world needs to be addressed. A tarnished public image is a liability hindering the contributions of the academy to society. Difficult and taxing as the economic problems are, they may not be the most serious threat to the future of higher education. The problem has been succinctly stated by The American Assembly program, the Integrity of Higher Education[1]:

> Public confidence in American higher education has been eroded in recent years. Consensus on what constitutes legitimate higher education has been reduced, and expectations of it—and claims for it—have not been fulfilled ... To be sure, the ethical behavior of educators may be neither better nor worse than that exhibited in the other professions. Perceived error causes demand for correction. Academic life carries for its members obligations of personal conduct (by trustees and administrators, faculty and students) that lift expectations of behavior beyond the ordinary. Unfortunately there are breaches of ethical conduct. Examples include plagiarism by both teachers and students; exploitation by faculty and administrators of graduate and teaching assistants; "double-dipping" by academic professionals from several grant sources for the same labor performed; undisclosed selling of identical scholarly works to more than one publication; the abject submission by institutions to groups who would deny open discourse on controversial subjects of interest to the campus community; withholding by college administrators of information that rightfully belongs to faculty and students; faculty departures from rigorous peer appraisal of colleagues; conflicts of interest among teaching, consulting, and publishing; grade inflation and unwarranted recommendations for students; and the unjustified imposition of prerequisites. There are many reasons why we should act promptly. In the first place, professors often act as critics of a society which grants substantial protections for this function. Such criticism will be ill-received if the professors' own house is in intellectual and moral disarray. Second, while instances of irresponsible behavior may be exceptional, the irresponsibilities of the few tarnish the good name of all. A third factor is that persistent irregularities may lead to yet greater abuses. Fourth, inaction from within will trigger greater control by public authorities. Fifth, all university and college personnel, by their practices and their conduct, may so profoundly affect the intellectual and moral development of the young that even seemingly minor departures from integrity cannot be tolerated.

Realistically and in the short run, all institutions could begin immediately a review of their policies relating to conflict-of-interest and consulting. It is recommended that faculty, administrators and governing boards initiate such studies, giving consideration to the following policy recommendations.

CURRENT UNIVERSITY POLICIES: POLICIES FOR CONSULTING AND CONFLICT OF INTEREST

Of immediate concern is the adequacy of existing policy. Our study of policies regarding consulting and conflict-of-interest at research and doctoral institutions indicated that although 96 percent of the responding institutions had policies (105 of 109 institutions), many of them did not have policies for specific issues.[2] It is concluded, however, that every institution should have policies covering all major aspects of consulting and conflict-of-interest. Although the specifics of the policy may vary to meet the needs of diverse and different institutions, it is recommended that the following should be included by all institutions:

Limitation of Time Spent on Consulting

A specific and unambiguous policy statement is recommended. The policy should be clear as to: a) the maximum time allowed, e.g., one day per week, with "week" defined; b) whether a weekly policy can be violated if a certain maximum number of days per quarter or semester is not exceeded, and, if so, under what circumstances; and c) the time period during which the policy is applicable, e.g., for academic year faculty from the first day of classes in the Fall through commencement in the Spring. If exceptions are allowable during holidays, e.g., Christmas and Spring vacation, the policy should be explicit. (At least one-third of the survey respondents do not now have policies which encompass these principles.)

Formal Approval Prior to Outside Appointments

A simple approval process for outside professional activities is recommended. The process should involve a brief written request stating the nature of the professional work, the name of the employing organization (if any), how the activity will benefit the faculty member and the home institution and the maximum amount of time to be spent. If the faculty member has a financial interest in the outside employer this should be stated. If there is a potential for conflict of interest this should be identified and a plan to avoid it outlined. Approval should preferably be with the departmental chairman or dean, and the process should be designed to avoid excessive delays. For cases where permission is denied, an appeal mechanism should be specified in the policy. If use of any university facilities is involved, proper approval should be secured. (At least one-quarter of the surveyed policies do not encompass these principles.)

Retrospective Disclosure of
Outside Professional Activities

A disclosure of all outside professional activities should be required on an annual or semi-annual basis. This statement should have a format similar to that of the approval form (e.g., for each outside appointment: name of employer, type of work done, time spent, how the activity benefited the faculty member and the institution). There is considerable controversy about disclosure statements, and whether they should be public information. Although we favor availability of disclosure statements to the public, the recommendation is limited to the policy requiring internal disclosure only. (Almost one-third of our surveyed policies do not address the elements in this recommendation.)

Use of University Materials, Facilities or the University Name

The policy should provide specifics for an approval process for use of university personnel, facilities or materials for any purposes that are not strictly university purposes. Exclusions, such as library, should be listed together with any limitations on the exclusion. Requests should be processed via a formal written form which provides information on the intended use, how it benefits the faculty member and the university and what compensation will be provided the university. Use of computer facilities for outside work can be handled through separate accounts paid by the individual users, and the policy should prohibit use of university paid computer facilities for personal gain. A specific policy statement prohibiting the use of the university name for outside commercial or other non-university purposes should be provided. Generally the use of university personnel, facilities or materials for outside non-university purposes should be discouraged. This suggestion does not preclude developing some very useful institutional-industry sharing of expensive facilities or sharing of employee costs, but it should be through the institution and not on a private or individual basis. (One-half or more of our survey respondents do not have policies that encompass these recommendations.)

Policy for Academic Year vs. Calendar Year Faculty

The extent to which policy constraints apply, if at all, to academic year faculty *during their summer free time* should be stated. Waiver of some specific approval policies for off-campus summer work of academic year faculty within the constraints of a general policy on responsible behavior is recommended. (Only 14 of our 98 respondents have a non-academic-year policy waiver and 11 have restrictions on outside activity during summer and leaves of absence.)

Policy should prohibit all types of conflict-of-interest activities. Accepting payment for tutoring, financial or other business relationships with institutional vendors (including accepting favors or gratuities) or other similar activities should be prohibited by policy. Earning royalties on textbooks or other educational materials used by students in the author's class or by other students at the author's institution should be prohibited. Such text materials could be sold, on the home campus, either at a royalty-free reduced rate or royalties could be given to the institution for scholarships or academic purposes. (In our survey, of 98 institutions only 19 had policy on gratuities, 24 on involvements with institutional vendors, and seven on tutoring. Data were provided by 39 institutions on copyright policy, of which only three forbade royalties on campus use of non-commissioned works and six on commissioned works.)

Teaching for Other Instituions,
Serving as Researchers on a Grant
or Contract for Another Institution

Policies are needed which specify under what circumstances, if any, teaching or research can be performed for an outside educational organization. We do not recommend any specific policy but suggest that every institution should have policy that covers these areas and that avoidance of conflict of interest should be an important object. (One-quarter of our survey respondents prohibit teaching at another institution, usually with the exception by specific written approval; we have no survey data on researchers.)

Full-Time Faculty or Staff Involvement
in Outside Companies

Involvement as founder, officer, consultant, stockholder or part-time employee in businesses related to the individual's university professional work has become an important issue on many campuses. At the time of our policy survey (1979) we did not find specific policies addressing this issue. The problems on many campuses, stemming from extensive off-campus business relationships related to campus professional work, indicate an urgent need for policy. It is therefore recommended that every campus

develop policy in this important area. The specific recommendations of the Ethical and Economic Issues Project will be found
later in this chapter.

Responsible Behavior

It is recommended that every institution have general policy
which governs outside faculty activity. Elements to be included
are: a) that the activity should be supportive of the institutional
goals; b) that it should add to or at least not discredit the
institution's image; c) that it should enhance the professional
status or skills of the faculty member; and d) that it should not
interfere with regular academic duties. (In our survey, two-thirds
had a non-interference policy, two-fifths had a professional en-
hancement policy, one-fifth an institutional goal policy, and only
14 an institutional image policy.)

Monitoring and Discipline

A process for monitoring and the disciplinary actions to be
taken for violation of policy should be written into the policy
documents. It is recommended that every institution provide monitoring and discipline procedures as components of its policy. (In
our survey one-fifth of the institutions had implement-
ing/monitoring policy and only one-tenth indicated disciplinary
actions for policy violations.)

Academic Ethics

Although all of these policy recommendations are related to
ethics, it is believed there is a need for specific policy dealing
with academic ethics. The policy recommendations are of the
nature of contracts—written stipulations of rights and duties
agreed upon by employer and employee. In addition a policy
statement that has more of the nature of covenant—relating to
the individual and collective responsibilities of the profession—is
proposed. The covenant approach will go beyond contract stipulations or self-interest and recognize the reciprocal obligations of all
those of academe toward each other while transcending the legalism of the contract approach.

ETHICAL AND ECONOMIC ISSUES

There are larger and more important issues which must be
addressed and solved. The academy has been given a special and
unique position in society as the primary repository, transmitter
and developer of knowledge. The imminent age of knowledge,
soon upon us, offers higher education the greatest challenge and

opportunity since the invention of the printing press. The traditions of unfettered thinking (academic freedom) and economic security through tenure, could, if practiced, provide the cornerstones for the academy to play a pivotal role in building the new knowledge society. But if the ethical basis for this important role in society is sold for short term economic advantage, both academics and all of society will be the poorer for it.

Ethical and economic issues are closely interrelated. Economic arguments, frequently of short term nature, are often used to justify questionable ethical behavior. The failure of academic year base salaries to keep pace with inflation provides justification for supplemental income work as economic necessity. Morale has also declined and decreased real dollar academic year salaries provides a rationale for reduced commitment to academic work. These tendencies must be overcome and attention focused on the positive, exciting future which we could create. Such an approach will help to improve the economic factors.

A summary analysis of important economic and ethical factors can provide the basis for longer range planning which, it is believed, would lead in the right direction.

Economic Factors

- The typical academic year faculty appointment (nine months) provides a base salary less than that earned by comparable non-academic professionals working a full year. However, if academic year salaries are increased to a full-time, full-year basis (an increase of 22-33 percent), they are generally competitive with those of comparable non-academic professionals.

- In recent years, academic year base faculty salaries have not increased as much as the increase of the CPI. Although this is also true for some other groups, faculty as a whole have had a serious erosion in the purchasing power of their base academic salaries.

- The majority of all faculty (80-90 percent) is engaged in one or more professionally related additional income activities, either for their own institution, outside, or both. These activities tend to make the academic position in total roughly equivalent in time commitment and earnings to similar non-academic professionals.

- Enrollments of traditional college-age undergraduates will decline over the next decade, making it more difficult to provide competitive faculty salaries if faculty size is to remain constant.

- The potential to faculty for very large economic gains from outside activities has become a temptation difficult to resist. Gene-splicing technology has received much recent publicity but there are many other examples. The million-dollar textbook royalty level is not unknown.

- Life-long learning of all forms will greatly increase as we become an information/learning society. However industry, proprietary and not-for-profit schools, and professional associations, will play an increasingly dominant role in adult teaching and learning, leaving a more minor role to colleges and universities. The reason for this is the second-class status of continuing education on most campuses. Faculty who teach in these programs generally do so on an overload salary basis and receive little or no other recognition for this work, no matter how important their contributions.

- Ownership and royalties on intellectual properties (patents, copyrights and works of art) are an important source of income for many faculty. The future potential for growth is excellent because of the new federal patent policy, the copyrightable status of software, and, in general, the technological explosion in electronic educational media. Most colleges and universities are not well prepared to deal with intellectual property issues or to turn them to the advantage of society.

- Faculty morale and sense of commitment to the purposes of their institution have probably declined both from resentment because of the decreased purchasing power of their base salaries and from the competition from other commitments needed to maintain earning power. This is an economic factor in the sense that quality of performance and productivity may be decreasing even when teaching loads may be mandated to increase.

Ethical Factors

- There is the serious conflict of interest in the allocation of professional time to basic academic work vs. additional income work. There is a loss of that precious "time to reflect" intended to accompany the traditional modest formal faculty teaching requirement. James Watson, who discovered the double helix, commented, "It's necessary to be slightly underemployed if you are to do something significant.[3] The number of faculty members even slightly underemployed has certainly decreased. There is also time pressure which causes neglect of informal contacts with students and colleagues, contacts which are of great value in high quality teaching and scholarship.

- Cognitive dissonance and the loss of academic freedom is now widespread. Unfettered intellectual inquiry and ability to state unpopular ideas becomes compromised by the vested interests related to additional earnings. Communications are inhibited because of needs for secrecy to protect ideas and information of potential commercial value or to be included in proposals for funding. These problems are generally unrecognized and occasionally vehemently denied.

- Loss of public credibility. The public senses conflict-of-interest situations and loses confidence in the objectivity of the academy. There is a suspicion that self-interest rather than public interest governs faculty actions. This credibility loss can have several negative impacts.

Most obvious is the decline in public financial support which means lower faculty salaries and more difficulty in developing new programs to meet changing societal needs. These negative factors, especially the faculty salary problems, will cause more faculty to seek supplemental income, thereby exacerbating the total problem. Outside financial interests which have the appearance of conflict-of-interest will undermine the usefulness of faculty expertise, especially in areas involved with important public policy issues.

These economic and ethical issues have evolved, largely by chance, from a combination of historical and political factors. It is not profitable to spend time in trying to affix blame or even if there be any—what is important is to carefully study what is needed to meet the goals of the academy. A far reaching discussion needs to be initiated keeping in mind that . . . "It is no longer possible to take the position that what is good for a university or for higher education is also good for society."[4] It is also unrealistic to take the position that what is good for the faculty is also always perceived as good for society. What appears to be urgently needed is an objective collection of facts, continuing the work begun in the Ethical and Economic Issues Project. The factors already identified . . . namely: 1) the part-time (academic year) nature of most faculty appointments; 2) the declining real base academic year salaries in recent years of high inflation (a trend which may have reversed starting in 1980-81); 3) the participation in extra income work, either for the home institution or outside (or both) by 80-90 percent of all faculty; 4) declining enrollments of traditional college-age students; 5) some cases of faculty earnings of hundreds of thousands or even millions of dollars from businesses and royalties derived from outside activities related to their academic work; 6) low status to life-long learning within academic circles and an increasing pre-emption of this growing field by non-university organization; 7) lack of comprehensive intellectual property policies which protect the integrity of academic institutions; 8) declining faculty morale and commitment to academic purposes; 9) conflict-of-interest in allocation of time to academic purposes vs. extra-income purposes; 10) cognitive dissonance and loss of academic freedom from economic pressures and secrecy in consulting, business ventures and grantsmanship; 11) a decline in public credibility and image. These factors all need to be considered and integrated into thinking about new and comprehensive faculty personnel policies.

A basic problem is the lack of definition of the role of faculty.

> Faculty members would like to regard themselves as auton-
> omous professionals operating under the banner of academic
> freedom to do what they please rather than justify their
> survival in terms of fulfilling social obligations. Their time
> reports reflect this view. [5]

In this same article Dressel points out that faculty reports of
time allocations to teaching, curriculum development, research,
public service, governance, advising and other functions are subjective, crude indicators at best, and that they provide no insight
into what faculty members should be doing. The fuzziness in
definition of what faculty *is* doing and what it *should be* doing
has consistently emerged as a major problem.

From a legal standpoint the role of full-time faculty, academic
or calendar-year, is that of an employee. State and federal laws
apply to faculty employees identically as to all other employees,
with one exception: full-time academic year faculty with continuing appointments are not permitted to draw unemployment insurance during the summer months even if they are unemployed.
This is true even if the employing institution's policy clearly
requires only nine months of service and the summer is free time
to be used completely at the discretion of the faculty member.
(However, we know of no institution that treats summer salary
paid to faculty on academic year appointments as overload salary.) Furthermore, government agencies which generally forbid
overload salary payments for work on sponsored projects *do not*
object to summer salary payments to these faculty; one agency
(National Science Foundation) has a limitation on summer salary
(2/9 of academic-year base) subject to occasional special exceptions.

The concept of faculty as autonomous professionals is in direct
contrast to that of the paid professional employee. If faculty really
are autonomous professionals, then the question remains: What
professional services are due the employing institution in exchange for the salaried, tenure-track position? Logically, part-
time faculty members who do not have a full-time position at any
institution appear to be closer to the autonomous professional
model. The part-time faculty member with no full-time position
seems almost identical however to the well accepted fee-for-service professional described earlier, a model which is distinctly at
variance with that of a full-time, tenure-track faculty member,
regardless of whether the appointment is academic year or calendar year.

A widely held concept of the faculty role is that of the responsible semi-autonomous professional. This concept holds that if a faculty member adequately teaches the courses assigned, performs satisfactory scholarship and does a fair share of student advising and university service *regardless of the time spent*, then the requirements of a tenure-track salaried position are satisfactorily met. This model rests on performance (output) and not on time spent (input). The primary problem with this model is that it requires the job to be sufficiently well defined that actual performance can be objectively measured against the position requirements. Rarely if ever is this the case. Indeed it seems likely that most faculty would rebel strongly against the rigidities of any job description adequate for the evaluation needs of this model.

Our reasoning leads us full circle. The dilemma is that academicians believe that the pursuit of ideas and the transmission of knowledge, especially in a society in great flux, is nurtured by an environment of academic freedom. Basically, there is a great reluctance to define the faculty role in any detail, for a more detailed definition, it is feared, would restrict free inquiry and cause more harm to the academy than any potential good. Clarification of the faculty role requires the perspective of the individual faculty as well as that of the institution and the society that supports it.

INDIVIDUALS, INSTITUTIONS, SOCIETY

Pluralistic values are prevalent within the university to as great or greater an extent than in any other modern institution. As in the history of democratic societies, there is hopefully a creative tension between those who seek to centralize and those who emphasize individualism. Pluralism enhances freedom but at the price of responsibility. George Bernard Shaw once wrote, "Liberty means responsibility. That is why most men dread it." In academe, individual liberty has not always been accompanied by the requisite commitment to responsibility. And even though the more flagrant cases involve a small minority, the impact on the public image can be large.

A recent survey[6] found that the most frequently mentioned quality the public seeks in leaders is honesty, followed (and not closely) by intelligence. This result implies that the public would also seek honesty (integrity) followed by intelligence in faculty and academic leaders. This should not be a difficult requirement since the two most prized qualities in academics are intellect and integrity. However the priority order may occasionally become reversed in academe, with intellect dominant over integrity. This should not be tolerated.

Much of university life can be regarded as an attempt to establish a quasi-socialist enclave within a capitalist society.* The problem may be viewed then as one of faculty expectation for the best of both the socialistic and the capitalistic worlds. This is an impossible goal, and it needs to be recognized as such. The freedom-responsibility relationship must be taken into account.

Academic freedom in scholarship is fundamental to the advancement of truth . . . and freedom is essential in teaching for the teacher and in learning for the student . . . Membership in the academic community also imposes responsibilities on faculty, students, administrators and governing boards . . . responsibilities for freedom of inquiry and expression, respect for the differing opinions of others, and a commitment to the defense of intellectual honesty.**

Academic freedom applies to the intellect—to the world of ideas and inquiry. To what extent, if any, should this freedom be available for the commercialization of intellect, for individual financial gain? It appears that as personal financial gain factors increase, intellectual academic freedom factors decrease. As profit potential becomes important it can channel and limit intellectual horizons, and ultimately the university will lose its most important and precious reason for being.

It is a special privilege to serve in an academic institution. There are rich life-long personal and professional rewards in learning and public service. Colleges and universities should seek talented and committed people as faculty and staff—people who share a vision of the intellectual excitement of teaching and discovery coupled with a dedication to service. However we must recognize that talented people are needed throughout our society in all occupations and professions. Not only are the talents of creative people urgently needed everywhere, but we must recognize that academic work has requirements other than high intellectual ability. Some of our faculty clearly have great entrepreneurial abilities in addition to their scholarly interests. Our free enterprise society needs these individuals—they make important contributions to the economy and can enhance our lives with new

---

* The author is indebted to Professor David Riesman, Harvard University, who provided this intriguing concept in a personal communication dated March 12, 1979.

** This statement is the author's paraphrased version of AAUP 1940 and 1970 statements.

and beneficial products and processes. However, the entrepreneurial role is inconsistent with that of the full-time academic person. There is an intrinsic conflict-of-interest between the two roles, academic and entrepreneurial: the academic seeks knowledge and learning for its own sake whereas the entrepreneur seeks to use knowledge and learning for financial gain. This is not to say that the entrepreneur has no role in academe; there is the important and useful role of adjunct, part-time appointments in which academic and entrepreneur could be complementary.

Thus, we conclude that the pluralism and freedom which should be strongly encouraged within academe should cover teaching, scholarship and public service—the world of ideas and the intellect—but *not* entrepreneurship. And we should make it clear that we are dealing here with professionally related businesses only (e.g., the professor of English who owns an apartment house is not an issue . . . although it could be if the time taken to manage the apartment interfered with faculty duties). The ideal faculty role would encourage unlimited intellectual freedom with applications to teaching, scholarship and public service—and in its purest form would prohibit entrepreneurship. It is concluded, then, that the unique faculty role requires a degree of commitment different from that in other salaried positions. In exchange for academic freedom, tenure and light formal work schedules the academic makes a commitment to scholarship, students and teaching and public service.

In order to realize the potential of the unique faculty role the institution (and society) must provide necessary support. Ideally the purpose of the institution is to provide the physical facilities and administrative organization to support the work of the faculty. Therefore the institution must strive to create an environment in which intellectual excitement will be constantly renewed and where academic freedom will flourish. The goal should be to recruit and retain talented and innovative people committed to teaching, scholarship and public service. Long-term financial stability of the institution is an essential characteristic to assure the economic security necessary for tenured appointments. And the need for truly full-time faculty appointments, with appropriate competitive salaries, cannot be overemphasized. The fact that most faculty today are on academic year appointments (nine-months or three-quarters time on an annual basis) is a major cause of the problems addressed in this monograph. Institutions have a responsibility to develop and sustain some full-time faculty positions, with salaries competitive with equivalent non-academic professionals. Institutional policy changes and reallocation of resources can help to achieve this goal. Improved public image could provide increased public support.

The academic ideal is envisioned, then, as a strong mutual commitment: on the part of the institution, to develop and maintain an environment of intellectual freedom, supportive of the best teaching, scholarship and public service, with the concomitant necessary long-term economic support; on the part of faculty and other employees, dedication to high standards in teaching, scholarship and public service, and maintenance of academic freedom, free from the pressures of commercialism and entrepreneurship. Although this ideal is difficult of attainment, we believe it to be a goal worthy of our best efforts. An important pathway to this goal is institutionalization of the academic profession.

Institutionalizing the Academic Profession

The traditional academic ideal involves a community of scholars as the core of the university . . . advancing the frontiers of knowlege . . . transmitting knowledge . . . and engaging in public service. Faculty were to monitor the decisions and behavior of administrators to insure that they were following the directions determined by the faculty. Equally or even more important, faculty were to monitor their own behavior. Peer pressure and review were to maintain high standards of academic conduct. However the increasing complexities of academic life, including the substantial involvement of faculty in outside ventures, has reversed the traditional roles. Now it has become the academic administrators who monitor faculty behavior for conflict-of-interest, performance of duties and unethical activities, and faculty generally are frustrated in their efforts to monitor or direct academic administrators. These changes are a real loss to the quality of academic life.

The current turmoil and fiscal crisis in higher education may provide an opportune time for institutionalizing the professoriate. By this is meant that faculty would devote their undivided attention to their own institutions and the attainment of their teaching, scholarly and public service goals through their institutional affiliations. Such faculty commitment could provide a healthy reform within institutions. Institutionalization of the professional implies that all those professional activities currently conducted outside the institution—teaching and research for others, industrial consulting, financial management involvement in businesses, etc.—these would all be conducted, if at all, through the institution and not on a personal—private basis.

This concept is not as revolutionary as may first appear. Much can be learned from medical practice plans.[7] More than one-half of all medical schools in the United States have a written practice plan which applies thoughout the school. In most of these plans all full-time clinical practitioners are required to belong. Although these plans are quite diverse, the majority centrally bill for all patient-generated income, and the income is used for expenses in operating the plan, for salaries (including incentive salaries in many cases), and for school purposes. The institution provides facilities, organization and management, thus freeing individual faculty to concentrate their efforts on their professional work. Faculty also have the benefit of a better and more stable income from the institution (including that of the medical practice plan). Malpractice insurance, which has been a difficult problem for individual practitioners or small groups, is provided by the institution. The institution benefits through sharing in the practice income and by the generally improved quality of environment resulting from total faculty professional commitment to the medical school's programs. With a professional practice plan, faculty participation in outside professional work would be more selective . . . based on professional factors and not on monetary gain. The public would not reject faculty expertise because of an apparent (or actual) conflict of interest—and faculty would be free to give their best intellectual effort without external economic pressure. Certainly the public image of the academy would improve under this system.

Experience with medical school practice plans would appear to be directly applicable to other professional schools. Most, if not all, of the problems resulting from faculty consulting could be solved by setting up practice plans in schools of engineering, business, architecture, education, etc. Just as there is great variation and complexity in the medical practice plans, so we would expect professional practice plans to vary, each perhaps with its own unique characteristics. "Grandfathering" would be necessary in some cases. Establishing a new professional practice plan might be facilitated by making participation mandatory for all newly appointed faculty, who would be familiar with and would accept the plan details prior to accepting appointment, and optional (at least for a limited period of time) to current faculty. The potential academic and financial benefits to both the faculty and the institutions are so large as to strongly encourage study and changes to overcome the opposition from the traditions of individual faculty entrepreneurship.

In 1944 the University of Chicago under Robert Hutchins instituted the so-called 4-E faculty contract, the terms of which required all outside earnings to be turned over to the university. At the time this plan as initiated faculty were given an exceptionally large salary raise. The plan was very controversial with both strong supporters and detractors. This type of contract was abandonded after Hutchins left Chicago in 1951. A survey of faculty under the 4-E contract indicated that this type of appointment did increase time commitment to the university and that faculty were more selective in their outside activities; a majority also felt that a 4-E or modified 4-E contract might be useful today.[7] Some felt that the 4-E was too idealistic and inflexible; ultimately, the inability of Chicago to keep up with post-World War II inflation, and the competitive faculty market forced Chicago to abandon the 4-E after Hutchins left. The current declining faculty market and societal attitudes toward conflict-of-interest in the decades of the eighties and nineties may be quite favorable for the development of contracts like the 4-E. It is recommended that colleges and universities consider various modified 4-E contracts as well as professional practice plans.

Fragmented Faculty Commitments and Earnings

The part-time nature (i.e., academic year) of faculty employment has been a thread running throughout these studies: part-time in basic salary, and part-time in the mutual commitment between faculty and their institutions. Institutions are reluctant to increase their fiscal commitments to their faculty, although they provide a large source of temporary employment to their own faculty in overload and summer teaching as well as sponsored research.

Institutions do not want to incorporate their share of these supplemental salaries into regular full-time salaried positions because of concern over the additional financial commitment. The current hodge-podge of sources of faculty earnings paid by the institution consists of what is euphemistically called "hard money" (base salary) and "soft money" (overload and summer salary). There is a growing recognition, however that the distinction is disappearing: the "hard" sources are "softening" at the edges. Unfortunately this trend increases the pressures to minimize institutional commitments to faculty salaries, a serious problem if overload or summer salaries are to be incorporated into academic year base salaries to make full-time positions.

There are other problems. Some faculty (about twenty-five percent are on full-time calendar year appointments. During campus interviews several administrators stated that calendar year faculty write fewer research proposals and are less productive. If this is true, it is a problem to be met by evaluation-review, and the promotion and tenure process, as with any other non-productive faculty member. Another criticism of the calendar-year appointment is that some faculty members believe that they receive no more salary for full-time service than their faculty colleagues who are on academic year appointments. Our data show that this is generally not true: the problem may be caused by discipline-based salary differences. For success of any full-time calendar year salary plan, however, it is *essential* that salaries be increased appropriately over those for academic year service. Furthermore it is not clear that current calendar year faculty are any less involved in external professional income-producing activities than academic year faculty.[9] Although more calendar-year faculty (16 percent) have no supplemental income than academic-year faculty (6 percent), more calendar year faculty report consulting as the first or second largest source of supplemental income (44 percent) than academic year faculty (32 percent).* Incorporation of full-time calendar year appointments into a professional practice plan would provide a solution to this problem.

Interviews with faculty and administrators on a number of campuses indicate another important problem. Many appear to have an unrealistic (and very generous) idea of the actual salaries earned by non-academic professionals. Quoted salaries frequently ranged from 50-200 percent above actual published salary data for the professions and may be based on very exceptional cases and not typical earnings. This problem could be addressed by campus dissemination of available data on non-academic professional salaries. At the same time some faculty confided that they would not leave academe because they could not afford the cut in income!

It is concluded that multiple sources of faculty income are undesirable. It is not necessarily the extra income activities that are intrinsically bad; in fact, many of them are useful and desirable. It is the supplemental income relationship to the basic academic activity and the fact that academic-year salaries are less than comparable full time non-academic professional salaries. These factors undermine the academic ideal.

In reality, colleges and universities have developed a myriad of appointments for instructional staff. Most are ad hoc, the exception being that of tenure-track appointments where rights and responsibilities are usually covered by faculty handbooks and other policy manuals. However, individuals with "faculty-like" characteristics are employed full and part-time to teach, do re-

*See Table 1, Chapter 4, Page 49.

search, administer, counsel, advise, and so on under many differing job titles and types of appointments. In many cases a primary object is to meet academic needs in these areas *without* increasing the institutional commitment to tenure-track regular faculty. It is not uncommon to find some of these non-faculty "faculty" actually performing more traditional faculty functions (in particular, teaching) than some of the full-time tenure-track faculty. This situation is quite relevant to the topics of this monograph because, as supplemental income activities of tenure track faculty increase their institutional commitment can decrease to the point that it is less than that of many of the part-time academics (some of whom aspire to full-time positions but whose appointments are non-tenure track). Aside from the obvious unfairness of this situation, the negative morale factors on all concerned cannot but have an adverse effect on institutional quality.

We conclude that colleges and universities have an urgent need to review and revise policies for appointments of all professional personnel who will be serving academic faculty-related functions. The approach needs to be comprehensive and open and should result in a codified, published policy document. Our studies suggest there is need for a range from truly full-time faculty to various types of fractional, part-time appointments. The institutional commitment to the individual and the reciprocal commitment by the individual to the institution should be directly related to salary and other benefits, both monetary and nonmonetary. Although there is a need for flexibility the current widespread ad-hocism has outlived its usefulness and needs to be replaced by carefully thought-out policy.

First and foremost, we believe that the academy needs a core group of competent, committed and productive academics who should be able to earn full-time, competitive professional salaries working for their own institutions. These truly full-time appointments would constitute the heart and soul of the institution, enjoying the full benefits of tenure and academic freedom. Such appointees should have the possibility of independent professional choice—independent of additional income—and they should be evaluated on their professional contributions to teaching, scholarship and service. In return the appointees would commit their full-time professional activities to the institution—all professionally related earnings would go to the institution (via a professional practice plan or a type similar to the Chicago-Hutchins 4-E contract). Support of a highly entrepreneurial faculty—no matter how outstanding it is—of men and women who use their institutional positions and academic freedom to amass private fortunes for themselves, is not consistent with the accepted role of the university of teaching, scholarship and service. Such entrepreneurial individuals can best serve the university in non-tenure track, adjunct faculty roles. It should be made clear that the objections are not to the amassing of wealth itself but to the twin problems of the impact on public attitudes about the university's service to society and the internal impact on the environment of intellectual freedom. The demoralizing effect of the money-oriented entrepreneurial faculty on those other faculty (of which there are many) whose energies are dedicated to academic goals, is not to be underestimated. The very special privileges bestowed by society on academic institutions were never intended to provide an opportunity for energetic and creative people to become wealthy. An additional potential concern is the tax free status of colleges and universities which could be jeopardized by faculty involvement in outside for-profit business ventures if too closely related to their university work.

We emphasize the need for these new "core" faculty appointments because we believe they are essential to the teaching/scholarship/service roles of the university. These appointments should be the most prestigious and sought-after positions—the highest honor the institution can bestow, perhaps patterned after chair type appointments. A range of other appointments (generally without tenure), classified by appropriate fractional time commitments and titles, needs to be developed. Although current models exist for a great number of adjunct, part-time, clinical, visiting and other types of "faculty-related" appointments, many are ad hoc. What is needed is thoughful consideration of the legal, economic and ethical considerations relating to the rights and responsibilities of each type of appointment. Institutional policy developed on the basis of such considerations should be developed, published and disseminated.

Lengthy campus discussion will certainly be required to develop and implement new types of faculty appointments, professional practice plans, new policies on intellectual properties and commercialization of university work. Campus discussions could be dominated by tenured, senior faculty, some of whom may feel that any new policies will be restrictive and a loss to them. The need to rise above narrow self-interest is urgent. Without reform from within it will be imposed from outside and is then less likely to be satisfactory. We hope that many faculty will recognize these needs and that it will be possible for them to develop faculty personnel policy adequate not only to faculty and their institutions but to the longer range and changing needs of society.

We all recognize that meaningful tenure commitment requires long-term fiscal stability. Public support of higher education has sometimes proved fickle. The reasons for changing public attitudes and support are not simple. Nonetheless we do suggest that in the long run more stable public support would result from institutional reform addressing the problems discussed in this monograph. We believe this would be true both for funding from taxpayers and for gifts that are tax-deductible. We sense that the public is seeking credibility, honesty, and commitment to long-range public interest and the institutions that move in directions enhancing these qualities can expect increased support.

Institutionalizing the professoriate will provide new income and enhance increased long-term fiscal stability according to the following proposals:

Government Funding   Consolidation of some government funding from small project grants/contracts into longer term step-funded block grants. Analysis suggests that this change could enhance faculty creativity and innovation while simultaneously increasing productivity. Such a move would provide more stable long-term support and could be used to provide faculty salary for the proposed full-time appointments.

Office of Intellectual Property Management (OIPM)   It is recommended that every university establish an OIPM. The functions of this office have been described in Chapter Six. The OIPM could deal broadly with all intellectual properties including artistic works, computer software (including CAI) and data bases, audio-visuals, TV productions, as well as the more conventional inventions-patents and copyrights for text books. There is an expanding opportunity for public service and income to the college or university from an OIPM.

Royalty Income   Congressional legislation now gives patent title to the institution for inventions from most sponsored research (about $5 billion per year). Academic purposes could be better served if the institution owned all intellectual property resulting from the professionally related work of faculty and all other employees. Royalty sharing on a sliding scale is the preferred recommendation, a larger percentage to the individuals when total royalties are low, decreasing to a small share as total royalties increase. A system is recommended where most (or all) royalty income accrues to the institution, coupled with a personnel evaluation/reward system (tenure, rank, salary) which recognizes inventions and copyrightable materials as creative works worthy of academic recognition on their own merit regardless of income generated.

Teaching The most important single source of supplemental income, teaching, is also the most important function of higher education, even at research universities. However data indicate that teaching is less rewarded than is research and outside professional activities.[10] It is recommended that teaching be given more recognition and that some of the current overload teaching, including summer teaching and continuing education be taken on-load. This would not be appropriate for all teaching but could easily be done for some programs. Implementation would undoubtedly increase teaching for some faculty members but, if they are outstanding teachers and are rewarded for teaching performance, the recommendation should be a viable one. For some faculty this could result in a truly full-time annual appointment, with teaching the primary function.

Industrial-University Research Federal funding of university research is not increasing, and government regulations are perceived to have increased. Rather suddenly, industry looks much more attractive as a source of research funding for universities. Concern centers on secrecy and infringements upon the free exchange of ideas essential to university scholarship. There are now a number of multi-million dollar research agreements between major industries and several research universities. Interviews conducted with investigators at some of these institutions[11] indicate that none of the participating institutions have adequately addressed issues relating to industrial consulting, conflict-of-interest and participation in industry-supported research at the university. Some faculty, engaged in outside consulting work, refuse to work on industry-supported university research because of potential conflict-of-interest and the possible loss of earnings from their external consulting activities. The West German chemical company Hoechst AG is funding a department of Molecular biology at Massachusetts General Hospital (MGH) for 10 years with a $70 million agreement. This agreement, initiated by Howard M. Goodman, makes Goodman the director of the new department, placing a great deal of responsibility and influence on one person. An analysis of the Hoechst agreement has been published[12]; Hoechst has exclusive funding rights, scientists will be regular members of the MGH staff (nominated for faculty membership at Harvard Medical School) whose duties will be primarily research for the department (with a "reasonable" amount of time for faculty duties other than research and for consulting for non-profits if such activities *do not* interfere with their research), publication can be held-up for 30 days for Hoechst review and patents will belong to MGH (but MGH will grant licences to Hoechst at royalty rates that give "due consideration" to the fact that Hoechst paid for the research).

There are a growing number of multi-million dollar industrial funding agreements with universities. Because these agreements are relatively new and it has taken some time before some institutions were willing to publicly release the detailed agreements, no detailed comparison analysis has been done. Nonetheless the new Monsanto-Washington University agreement appears to be the best current model.[13] This contract is an "institution-institution" agreement, "quite deliberately drafted to deviate from the majority of arrangements in which corporate funds are earmarked for research by one or two senior investigators of the company's choosing." Funds will be dispersed by an internal granting agency; it is hoped that this mechanism will alleviate "elements of divisiveness" that may crop up when one or two superstars control large corporate funds. Another novel feature of the Monsanto-Washington University agreement is the "true partnership" relationship whereby many company scientists may be working on campus with university scientists—as full collaborators (how potential problems from this relationship will be avoided is not yet clear). Patents will be held by the University which will license Monsanto to develop them (exclusive licenses only when all funds were from Monsanto)—royalties paid to Washington University will be disbursed to the school, departments and laboratories and in *no case* will individual faculty receive any personal financial reward. Industry funding is a rapidly developing field which offers much potential over the next decade if carefully developed.

Professional Practice Plans With Medical Practice Plans as a model (and the Hutchins Chicago 4-E Contract) it is proposed that institutions experiment with the establishment of professional practice plans. As outlined earlier consulting and for-fee public service professional services would be conducted through the institution providing a source of income to the institution, schools and departments. It should be emphasized that although these professional practice plans will provide income to the institution their primary purpose is to provide a supportive environment for academic freedom and thereby enhance both the transmittal and development of new knowledge and public service. Implementation of professional practice plans is essential, it is believed, to improve the credibility and usefulness of faculty expertise and support the integrity of the academy. The income generated will help support the long range fiscal stability of the institution and provide resources for the full-time competitive faculty salaries which are considered to be very important in achieving those goals.

The Learning-Knowledge-Information Society

The electronic revolution is only just at its beginnings. At stake is not only the relative roles of various institutions in developing and meeting the needs of this new society—but much more importantly the very nature of this new and evolving era will depend on which interests are to dominate. Colleges and universities, at least in principle, have the potential and the ideal to look more objectively to the longer range best interests of society. This is a critical role and heavy responsibility which is not being met very well even though urgently needed. It is suggested that higher education should take more responsibility, using all available and developing electronic technologies, for life long education both for professional currency and the more general education necessary in a democratic society. As cable-TV expands the opportunities and needs for educational programs will expand—documentaries, critical issues, cultural and general education—the horizons are almost unlimited. If colleges and universities are to play a major role in these developments, in contrast to the more commercial development, a full-time, creative, competent and competitively paid faculty will be necessary. Such a faculty is possible and ideas for creating such a faculty have been proposed throughout this monograph.

In a recent article Thomas Mulkeen made the following observations:

> It is now becoming clear that the ever-expanding supply of educated workers is running up against a ceiling of job demand. Some observers have suggested that from an economic standpoint the value of an investment in a college degree has diminished. The world of work has undergone a far-reaching metamorphosis. The most striking change has been in the technical and managerial fields where new positions demand highly technical skills beyond the level offered by most college programs. Our mature, complex economic system has become dependent on the technology we have developed... The new electronic, biological, nuclear, and solar technologies are dramatically altering our society. The colleges and universities, part of the larger revolution that transformed our nation from an agrarian to an industrial power, are not now changing rapidly enough to keep pace with the technological age. The typical curriculum of the American college has not changed substantially since the turn of the century. Thus, at a time when education has consolidated its role in training, socializing, and selecting the work force, the curriculum remains entrenched in the past. The impact of

technology on the workplace, the changing circumstances of physical resources, the rise of new social expectations, and the dramatic new participation of women in the labor market have resulted in a disjuncture between what is expected in the workplace and what college graduates are prepared to do. Degrees become insignificant in a world in which skills are quickly outdated. The apparent inability of schooling to meet new training needs has led many employers to take on a larger share of the training function. Bell Telephone alone spends more than $700 million a year on training, and a host of new institutions offering specialized training programs have been organized in recent years.[14]

In this rather bleak assessment, Mulkeen sees colleges and universities playing a receding role in a society steps ahead of it. The facts indicate that industry, commerce and cultural organizations are increasingly finding ways to teach, inculcate and provide artistic and cultural experiences where higher education is either inadequate, out-of-date or simply not interested. The irony is that some of this learning is through moonlighting of college and university faculty and much of it can trace its beginning to research and teaching from the academy.

Society also has a growing need for information — for data bases and studies which can help make better decisions more favorable to our future. The expertise of the academy could be a great asset. As an example a recent report[15] stated that the American Telephone Company and affiliates paid almost $3.5 million to hundreds of professors in 1981 for consulting, economc studies and expert testimony. The fees ranged from almost a quarter of a million dollars (to a Stanford economics professor and a business associate) to a little more than a thousand dollars. Obviously the government antitrust case and the proposed divestiture of A. T. and T. involves technical and economic policy of great interest and concern to the general public.

The university has the expertise, the public need for credible data, analyses and advice is frequently urgent and resources are available to pay for the professional services. Our recommendation for a professional practice plan would make it possible for the faculty to have full-time positions, at competitive salaries, free of the financial and administrative pressures exerted by private consulting work and external business ventures.

Some of these full-time faculty might devote themselves entirely to teaching—undergraduate, graduate and professional students and life long learning programs. The creative energies of such faculty would be fully available for educational innovations such as production of TV documentaries on critical issues, application of research on learning to the teaching program, and experimentation such as with computer instruction.

At this critical junction in our history, colleges and universities face the greatest intellectual challenges since the dawn of history. It is both the best and the worst of times—difficult but exciting and requiring bold new thinking . . . building on the many good ideas of the past. As quoted at the beginning of this monograph, Henry Pritchett, then president of the Carnegie Foundation for the Advancement of Teaching, wrote in 1908 [16]:

> Extra-university employment should never be forced upon teachers by a salary schedule arranged on a part-time basis. College and university teaching is sufficient to employ to its full capacity the energy of a single mind.

And later in 1919, John D. Rockefeller, in his letter of conveyance with $50 million to the General Education Board wrote:

> It is of the highest importance that those entrusted with the education of youth and the increase of knowledge should not to be led to abandon their calling by reason of financial pressure or to cling to it amid discouragements due to financial limitations.

This monograph was written because the authors believe strongly in the purposes of the academy. We have tried to make our criticisms positive and constructive. The suggestions and recommendations for change are intended as starting points for wider discussion leading to additional and hopefully better ideas. We feel that those of us working within the proverbial academic vineyards hold an almost sacred trust—to study, and think and learn—and to change ourselves appropriately as we contribute to the rapid changes in the world around us. And to put the interests of society and of our institutions above those of our own self-interest. To do less is not worthy of the trust which has been given to us.

References

1   "The Integrity of Higher Education," *The American Assembly Program* (Columbia University, March 1979).

2   Dillon, Kristine E. and Bane, Karen L. "Consulting and Conflict of Interest," *Educational Record,* LXI, No. 4, Spring 1980, pp. 52-72.

3   Judson, Horace *The Eighth Day of Creation.* (New York: Simon and Schuster, 1979), p. 20.

4   Dressel, Paul, "The Shaping of Institutional Research and Planning," *Research in Higher Education,* XIV (No. 3) 1981, p. 246.

142 | 5   *Ibid.*, p. 233.

  6   "Connecticut Mutual Life Report on American Values in the 80's: The Impact of Belief" Connecticut Mutual, 140 Garden St., Hartford, CT 06115 (1982). Excerpts published in *AAHE Bulletin,* Vol. 34, No. 6 (February 1982).

  7   "Medical Practice Plans at U.S. Medical Schools. A Review of Current Characteristics and Trends" Vol. I and Vol. II Association of American Medical Colleges, One Dupont Circle, N.W., Washington, D.C. 20036 (1977).

  8   Survey of the Chicago 4-E Contract. Robert H. Linnell, Office of Institutional Studies, University of Southern California, Los Angeles, CA 90089. Results based on 12 responses from faculty who served at Chicago under the 4-E contract.

  9   Marsh, H.W., "Total Faculty Earnings, Academic Productivity and Demographic Variables," Fourth Annual Academic Planning Conference, University of Southern California, Institutional Studies, Los Angeles, CA 90089. June 11-13, 1979.

  10 Marsh, H.W., *op. cit.*

  11 Linnell, Robert H. "Business/Higher Education Research Partnerships" National Conference on Higher Education, American Association for Higher Education. Washington, D.C. March 5, 1981.

  12 Culliton, Barbara J., "The Hoechst Department at Mass General" *Science* CCXVI (June 11, 1982), pp. 1200-1203.

  13 Culliton, Barbara J., "Monsanto Gives Washington U. $23.5 Million," *Science* CCXVI (June 18, 1982) pp. 1295-1296.

  14 Mulkeen, Thomas A. "Higher Education in the Coming Age of Limits: An Historical Perspective" *Journal of Higher Education* Vol. 52, No. 2, pp.310-316 (May/June 1981).

  15 Watkins, Beverly T. "Telephone Company Paid $3.5 Million to Hundreds of Professors in 1981" *The Chronicle of Higher Education,* Vol. XXIV, No. 16, June 16, 1982.

  16 Pritchett, Henry "The Financial Status of the Professor in America and Germany" Bulletin No. 2, p. VII, the Carnegie Foundation for the Advancement of Teaching, New York, May 1908.